MW00438952

Unlocking the Annuity Mystery

Practical Advice For Every Advisor

Scott Stolz, CFP®, RICP®

No part of this book may be reproduced, stored in a retrieval system, or transmitted by any means without the written permission of the author.

CONTENTS

INTRODUCTION

After finishing graduate school in 1983, Edward Jones was good enough to offer me a job as an Annuity Product Manager. My first thought was "that sounds pretty cool," followed very quickly by "what *is* an annuity?" Still in the scholastic frame of mind, I simply assumed I could pick up a book or two on the subject and get up to speed quickly. The only problem was that there were no books on annuities – not even an "Annuities For Dummies". Fortunately, annuities were much simpler back then, so it was not terribly difficult to learn the product line. There were no enhanced death benefits or living benefits. There was only one variable annuity on the market and there were no indexed annuities or structured annuities. Financial institutions pretty much sold just one annuity at the time – a fixed annuity offered by two insurance subsidiaries of Baldwin United. If you are wondering if that could be connected in any way to the piano company of the same name, wonder no more. It was. And for those of you that were not in the industry back then, well, let's just say that those annuities hit a flat note. But I digress.

The point is that annuities are much more complicated, and flexible, now than they were in the mid-1980s. This truth hit me last year when I stumbled across a copy of the 1947 edition of a book series entitled "Modern Business" on the shelves of a vacation house my family had rented. One of the approximately 20 books in the series was entitled "Insurance" and was written by Bruce D. Hudgett, Ph.D., an economics professor at the University of Minnesota[i]. The section on annuities covered an entire 2-½ pages and dealt only with immediate annuities. I found it particularly interesting to note that even back then the author misrepresented how to calculate the return on an immediate annuity when he stated that a $69.66 a year payment on a $1,000 life only annuity provided an "...apparent return for the money invested is 6.966%". I'll give the esteemed Dr. Hudgett the benefit of the doubt and assume he meant that it provided a 6.966 percent cash flow rather than an actual yield, but regardless, it makes the point of how easy it can be to incorrectly describe how an annuity works.

Of course, today there are numerous books and articles on annuities – including the aforementioned "Annuities for Dummies". While some of these books are quite informative, I find that most of them are heavy and dense. They read too much like textbooks or get mired in the mechanics of the annuity contract, or both. This handbook was written for the advisors and agents that currently utilize, or are considering utilizing, annuities in their practice. Therefore, the focus is on how to properly position the various kinds of annuities in a client's portfolio. Perhaps more importantly, I have attempted to clearly articulate when annuities may produce less than the desired result – something that advisors are rarely told, I find. Yet, it is these very situations that can give advisors and their clients the most heartache.

Not too long ago, annuities were sold primarily for their tax-deferred growth benefits. That meant the policies required minimal maintenance and oversight after the policy was issued. If it was a fixed annuity, the advisor only had to pay attention to the renewal rates and the surrender charge period. If it was a variable annuity, the advisor mostly had to be concerned with the allocations within the sub-accounts. Given all of the riders and features that exist on annuities offered today, I would argue that properly managing an existing annuity has become a difficult and time-consuming process. Yet very few insurance companies offer much assistance in this area and broker-dealer back offices are typically not staffed to provide the necessary support. Therefore, this handbook allocates significant space to suggestions on how to manage today's extensive annuity features after the policy is issued. I'm guessing that some of my advice will surprise you. I'm also guessing that some of it will seem so logical that you will wonder why no one had told it to you before.

I also strive for objectivity and balance, exploring the caveats of annuities so thoroughly at times that you might wonder if I'm for or against them. Having been involved in the annuity business in a multitude of capacities for over 35 years, I can assure you that I am definitely a fan of annuities. Any investment vehicle that allows policyholders to grow an unlimited amount of money without receiving a 1099-and can provide you a personal pension for life is very appealing, obviously. However, over the years I have seen far too many situations where advisors have tried to utilize annuities as a panacea to address a wide range of financial situations. And of course, the insurance companies that sell annuities rarely go out of their way to dissuade advisors from being too aggressive in their application of an annuity as a financial tool. I, therefore, do not find it surprising at all that annuities are one of the most controversial financial products offered today. People seem to either love annuities or hate them. Those that love annuities are often blinded by the product's limitations, thereby giving more fuel to those that hate annuities. Yet I find that those that hate annuities are often ignorant about many key aspects of annuities. The truth is typically somewhere in the middle for a product that is so polarizing. This book sets out to establish some balance in the debate. It will provide a litany of applicable methods to help clients' achieve their financial goals, but I do not hesitate to point to where I think a bright line should be drawn between wise and irresponsible annuity strategies.

Financial advisors and agents who sell annuities make up the core audience for this book, but many more people can benefit from this information. I have tried to strike a fair and balanced tone here, which will, hopefully, be useful to individuals that already own annuities or are considering incorporating them into their investment portfolios. With this in mind, I have tried to limit the financial jargon to a minimum and deliver a clear and conversational message about these products.

Finally, given my current capacity at Raymond James Financial, I should state for the record that the opinions in this handbook are solely mine and don't represent the views or opinions of Raymond James (I can hear the lawyers thanking me now). I hope you find this book to be useful to you in some way.

---

[i] "Insurance" by Bruce D. Mudgett, Ph.D., Professor of Economics, University of Minnesota. In collaboration with Edward R. Hardy, Ph.B., Secretary-Treasurer, Insurance Institute of America; Solomon S. Huebner, Ph.D., Sc.D., Professor of Insurance and Commerce, University of Pennsylvania; Dean of the American College of Life Underwriters; G.F. Michelbacher, M.S., Vice President and Secretary, The Great American Indemnity Company. **Modern Business**, A Series of Texts prepared as part of the Modern Business Course and Service. *1947 Edition. Copyright, 1940, 1941, 1942, 1943, 1944 by Alexander Hamilton Institute Incorporated.*

CHAPTER 1
FIXED ANNUITIES

What is there to say about fixed annuities? Find a good interest rate from a solid company that offers decent service and has a history of renewing contracts at a fair rate of return. There's really not much more to fixed annuities than that. In fact, I considered ending this chapter after just that first sentence. But there are a few nuances that should be considered. Let me preface the remaining comments by first saying that this chapter deals only with traditional fixed annuities. While indexed annuities are indeed a fixed annuity, given some of the unique characteristics of the product, you will find them covered in a separate chapter.

1. What is the true rate guarantee and surrender charge period?

When it comes to how interest is credited on the policy, fixed annuities come in three flavors. The easiest structure to understand and explain is one that resembles a CD. It offers a multiple year rate guarantee that matches the length of the surrender charge. These are sometimes referred to as rate-to-maturity contracts or multiple year guarantee annuities (MYGAs). The beauty of these fixed annuities is that you can tell the client exactly how much money he or she will have at the end of the interest rate guarantee, at which point, you then shop for another annuity if you don't like the renewal rate on the existing annuity.

The second type of fixed annuity is one that offers a rate guaranteed for one year and then provides a renewal rate each year thereafter. Since these annuities typically have surrender charge (early withdrawal penalty) for seven years or longer, you have to trust the insurance company is going to treat the policyholder fairly after the first year. Often times these fixed annuities will offer an artificially high initial rate in order to attract the policyholder. This isn't necessarily bad as long as the insurance company has a history of paying competitive renewal rates. Always get a renewal rate track record before recommending one of these annuities.

The final type of fixed annuity is one that is between the first two. It will offer a rate guarantee for more than one year, but less than the length of the surrender charge. Perhaps it will guarantee a rate for three years, but still have a seven-year surrender charge period. Often, the insurance company will guarantee a minimum renewal rate that is higher than the contractual minimum rate until the end of the surrender charge period. Like the CD type annuity, because there is a known minimum rate of interest each year, you can quote a minimum value to the policyholder at the end of the surrender charge period. While this doesn't mean that the initial rate will be reduced to the quoted minimum, it's always best to sell the annuity based on that minimum. This allows you to prepare the policyholder for a worst-case scenario.

2. How does the insurance company calculate market value adjustments?

Rate-to-maturity contracts often come with a market value adjustment (MVA). While the MVA formula itself can be quite complex, the main thing you need to understand is that if the policyholder gets out of the contract prior to the end of the surrender charge period, the value of the annuity will be adjusted up or down based on the change in interest rates as compared to a stated index. If interest rates have increased, the policyholder's annuity value will be reduced when a withdrawal above the allowed free withdrawal is made. The opposite is true if interest rates fall. Generally, speaking, the policyholder's value will be increased if interest rates fall. The MVA allows the insurance company to at least partially hedge against a change in interest rates. In order to guarantee a rate for multiple years, the insurance company must invest the policyholder's premium in bonds with a maturity that is at least as long as the interest rate guarantee. Should the policyholder cash in the contract prior to the end of the initial rate guarantee, the insurance company could be exposed to interest rate risk if it has to sell the bonds that support the annuity prior to maturity. The surrender charge only serves to recover the upfront cost at issue – mostly the commission that is paid. It is not structured to absorb interest risk of the underlying bond portfolio. The positive of the MVA is that this "hedge" typically allows the insurance company to offer a more competitive interest rate. If the contract does not carry an MVA, then the initial rate must reflect this risk.

While this simplistic MVA explanation will suffice as a means to explain the concept to clients in most situations, there are occasions when a more specific explanation will be necessary. Some MVA formulas will create a negative MVA (which will reduce the account value on surrender) even if interest rates are up to 0.5% lower than the initial rate. Such a formula gives the insurance company a little extra buffer and therefore can help with the initial pricing. Because of this possibility, it is very important that you take the time to understand how a particular MVA formula works. At the very least, make sure you ask the insurance company if the MVA can ever be negative even if rates don't go up.

3. What is the value of bailouts?

Annuities that offer an unknown renewal rate, will sometimes offer a "bailout" rate. This feature says that if the renewal rate is less than the "bailout" rate, the policyholder can cash in the contract without being assessed a surrender charge. In other words, the policyholder can "bailout" and receive the full value of the contract. As an example, the initial rate might be set at 4.5% and the bailout might be 3%. This feature sounds attractive, but it provides more peace of mind than it does actual value. The insurance company incurs significant marketing, commission and policy issue expenses to put a policy on the books. The surrender charges are designed to recover those costs should the policyholder get out of the contract early. Simply put, it's not in the company's financial interests to allow the policyholder to cash out the policy before these initial costs can be recovered. Therefore, the insurance company is going to break the bailout rate only if interest rates have dropped enough to require them to do so. If that occurs, it is highly unlikely that the policyholder will be able to find another fixed annuity that pays more than the renewal rate being offered by the insurance company. Despite this, policyholders do like the idea that they have the option to get out if the renewal rate falls too much. Also, since the insurance company will not want to break the bailout, it will be motivated to pay at least the bailout rate even if rates in general have fallen.

4. Is a return of premium worth a look?

Since the surrender charge is always greater than the first year's interest rate on a fixed annuity, a policyholder will receive in return less than the initial premium only if he or she cashes out the contract in the first 12-18 months. While this can be looked at as similar to the "penalty for early withdrawal" that comes with CDs, most clients simply don't like the idea of getting back less than they had originally invested. These clients should therefore look for a fixed annuity that guarantees a return of premium even if the annuity is cashed in early. Not surprisingly, this feature comes at the cost of a lower interest rate. While the insurance company knows that few will take advantage of this feature, it must still set the initial rate assuming that a certain percentage of the policyholders will do just that.

Maintain a Three-Deep Bench

An insurance company's appetite for new fixed annuity business will change based on changes in interest rates, sales goals and internal capital needs. Since fixed annuities are essentially commodities, insurance companies know that they can quickly alter sales levels simply by increasing or decreasing interest rates relative to the competition. Therefore, your favorite company today could make itself uncompetitive tomorrow. For this reason, you should never rely on a single company as your go-to fixed annuity resource. Always take a few extra minutes to check with your home office or independent marketing organization to find out which fixed annuity company is trying to buy business, and is willing to do so by paying a slightly higher rate than the competition.

Summary

Given that approximately $30 billion per year is sold in fixed annuities, it feels like this chapter should be much longer. But to be honest, there's not much to say about fixed annuities and I pretty much said it all in the first sentence of this chapter. Assuming you are working with a financially sound insurance company, it really is mostly about the rate and the length of the surrender charge. Once you determine which of those two aspects are most important to your client, your choices become very simple.

CHAPTER 2
INDEXED ANNUITIES – THE REAL STORY

No other annuity elicits more polarizing opinions than indexed annuities. Some people lionize them as the best annuity creation ever, while others think they represent everything that is wrong with the financial services industry. If you are looking for me to break the stalemate in this chapter, I am sorry to disappoint you, because both opinions have strong merits, depending upon the product design of the annuity in question.

For the record, I'm a believer in what indexed annuities can deliver to clients. I joined Jackson National Life just before the company introduced one of the industry's first indexed annuities in 1997. That experience gave me a front row seat to the evolution of this type of annuity. While I believe that an indexed annuity can find a place in many conservative investors' portfolios, I also believe that, of the last 20 years, it is one of the most incorrectly sold financial products. Much of the blame for this rests with the insurance agents and financial advisors who have attempted to position these products as the answer to everyone's financial problems. The insurance companies, more so, carry a significant share of the responsibility: they have developed and marketed far too many indexed annuities that are designed to enrich the selling agent as much or more than the individual buying the annuity. The insurance industry learned long ago that higher commissions lead to higher sales. While the average commission on indexed annuities has steadily declined, relative to other types of annuities, too many indexed annuities still pay significantly more commission. Responsibility for this reaches state-level insurance authorities, too. As much as state insurance departments challenge the suitability of certain index annuities, these products could not exist unless those very entities approved them for sale. Any state insurance department that believes a surrender charge schedule of 15 years or more is rarely an appropriate product choice could have simply not approved the product for sale in its state. Fortunately, all of this continues to change.

We stand a slim chance of resolving any debate around the suitability of indexed annuities, to universal satisfaction. To understand indexed annuities, let us start with what they are *not*. **An indexed annuity is not an equity investment in any way and should NEVER be sold as an alternative to stocks, mutual funds or variable annuities.** The practice of substituting equity investments for indexed annuities is, without question, the greatest sin of many agents that sell indexed annuities – particularly agents that do not have a securities license. As the old saying goes, if the only tool you have is a hammer, everything looks like a nail. Given the poor equity returns in the first decade of this century, it became easy for agents and marketing organizations to assert that indexed annuities would deliver better returns over that 10-year period. Bold rallying calls like "capture the upside of the market, without the downside!" became common. All of this is absolutely wrong. An indexed annuity belongs in the fixed income sleeve of a client's portfolio. It is not, and never will be, an equity equivalent and should never be positioned that way!

If an indexed annuity is not an equity investment, then what is it? First and foremost, the product is just another form of a fixed annuity. In fact, they are now typically referred to as fixed indexed annuities. At the outset, these products were typically referred to as "equity" indexed annuities. However, as insurance companies and distributors began to make earnest efforts to improve the percentage of suitability sales, the "equity" part of the name was dropped in favor of the much more accurate description, "fixed". For the purposes of this book, I will refer to them as indexed annuities.

The only real difference between a traditional fixed annuity and an indexed annuity is the way that insurance companies calculate the credited interest. Essentially, rather than credit a specific rate of interest on the contract each year, the insurance company credits a rate based on the performance of an index. Most insurance companies utilize the S&P 500 as the measuring index. However, in an attempt to differentiate themselves, many insurance companies are also offering hybrid indices. No matter the index, over the long run, in exchange for giving up a known rate of return found in a traditional fixed annuity, the policyholder should expect to earn one to two percent more per year *on average* than a traditional fixed annuity over the course of the contract.

To qualify as a fixed annuity and not be considered a security, all indexed annuities must guarantee a minimal rate of interest. Contracts issued when interest rates were higher offered more generous minimum rates – sometimes as much as one to two percent per year. In today's interest environment, it may be as little as two percent on 87.5 percent of the original principal. It's easiest to just think of the contract as guaranteeing the policyholder's principal or just a little more after the contract has been in force five to seven years. Because the insurance company just has to essentially return the policyholder's principal, they don't need to invest the policyholder's entire premium into fixed income securities. They just need to invest enough of the premium to grow to the guaranteed amount in year 5-7. That leaves part of the premium available to use to purchase options on the underlying index. Graphically, a policyholder's premium might be divided as follows:

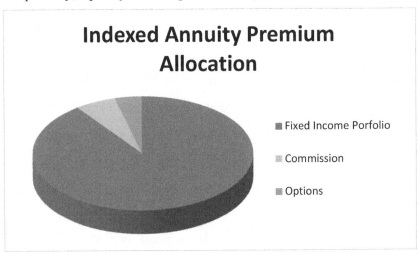

Indexed Annuity Premium Allocation

- Fixed Income Porfolio
- Commission
- Options

If an insurance company were investing for a traditional fixed annuity, the option slice of the pie would simply be added to the fixed income portfolio so that the insurance company could credit a specific rate of return. I will also note that there is nothing magical about using an index such as the S&P 500. The insurance company could use any asset that they could hedge. In fact, I've often half kiddingly suggested to several index annuity carriers that they would have great success selling an indexed annuity that had a rate of interest tied to the performance of a specific sports team. Such a design could mostly certainly be hedged in Las Vegas rather than Wall Street. And who wouldn't want to earn additional interest whenever their favorite college football team wins a game? But I digress.

You will note how the options slice of the pie is a small portion of the total premium paid. These products are not designed to give the policyholder the full upside of the index. In this interest rate environment, there simply is not enough money available to buy enough options to fund anything except a portion of the index return – especially in years when the market goes up significantly. You can also see how higher interest rates can produce higher potential returns. If an insurance company can invest the fixed income portion of the pie at eight percent rather than four percent, less money is needed to provide the minimum guarantee offered by the contract. That leaves more money to purchase options, essentially expanding that slice of the pie. This, in turn, allows the insurance company to more closely match the returns of the underlying index.

I can't stress enough, however, that a policyholder should never be led to believe that they would capture all or even most of the market upside. It is possible that there could be years where some crediting methods can provide much of the market upside, but those years will be few and far between. In addition, during periods of poor equity markets such as the lost decade of 2000-2009, there can be lengthy periods when an indexed annuity would provide a higher annual return than a true equity investment. But this would be equally true for other fixed income investments. The objective of these products is to offer a better return than other principal-protected investments – not match stock market returns.

Are There Fees or Not?

As if casting indexed annuities in the role of understudy for equity investments wasn't enough work, now we have to dispel yet common misconception about the product. "Index annuities have no fees," is the most common answer to questions about costs. But let's be realistic here. The insurance company is not giving the product away, so there are most certainly fees built into the product. Yet the way they accomplish this can give the impression that the products do not charge a fee. The correct answer to the question about fees is:

"Like a fixed annuity or a CD, index annuities are spread products. The fees and profit margin are built into the quoted rates."

Another way to put it is that there are no explicit fees charged to the policy (unless you add a living or enhanced death benefit). But it would be misleading to imply to the client that he or she would be paying no fees on an indexed annuity.

Crediting Methods

Crediting methods determine the amount of interest that should be credited to annuity products. The crediting methods vary widely, thereby adding to the perceived complexity of these products. Over the long run, they are all likely to provide similar returns. No matter which crediting method is selected, they all are supported by the same pie chart as the one above. In other words, if each of the crediting methods were funded by the same option budget, why would you expect any one method to return more than the others over the long run?

An indexed annuity policyholder is likely to ask you lots of questions during the course of the contract. One of the most likely will be why he or she earned the percentage that they did. It's very important that you can answer this question in the clearest and most direct terms. Since indexed annuities without living benefits cannot decline in value from year to year, you don't have to worry about the client complaining about the value falling in value. If you have sold a consumer-friendly contract, the policyholder would have to surrender the contract within a year or two after the policy is issued in order to lose money. They will complain, however, if the interest credited does not meet their expectations. And it's hard for a policyholder to have realistic expectations if he or she doesn't understand how interest is credited to the contract. Therefore, I always recommend sticking with the three simplest crediting methods.

1. Annual Point-to-Point with a Cap: Recommended

With the annual point-to-point crediting method, the insurance company looks at the value of the underlying index on each policy anniversary, then calculates the return using the change in the value of the index over the full year. This method always comes with an annual cap, which is the most the contract is required to credit in any given year. The size of the cap depends on interest rates and the price of the underlying options. The higher interest rates usually mean, the higher the caps. Similarly, the cheaper the value of the cost of the options, the higher the cap. Let's look at two simple examples – one where the market goes up and another where it goes down.

Example #1: Market goes up
S&P 500 Index value on policy issue date: 1500
S&P 500 Index value on 1st policy anniversary: 1650
The insurance company is guaranteed to credit the change in the index up to a cap of five percent.

In this example, the index goes up exactly ten percent ((1650-1500)/1500). Since the cap is five percent, the policyholder will earn five percent. Had the index gone up four percent to 1560, then the policyholder would earn the full 4%. This is a good time to point out that the index return does not include dividends. Only the absolute change in the price of the index is used. This is yet another reason why index annuities will not provide stock returns similar to equities over the long run.

You can see how simple this method is. This is particularly true if the contract uses an index that is readily quoted each day such as the S&P 500.

Example #2: Market Downturn
S&P 500 Index value on policy issue date: 1500
S&P 500 Index value on 1st policy anniversary: 1400
The insurance company is guaranteed to credit the change in the index up to a cap of five percent.

With this method, the policyholder will not be credited any interest in years where the index declines in value. Will the policyholder be disappointed? Of course. No one wants to earn zero percent in any year. In a year when the stock market went down, however, it is likely that many of the policyholder's other holdings dropped in value. Relatively speaking, assuming the contract was sold correctly, the policyholder will often be the most satisfied with the index annuity in down years. In fact, the greater the size of the market decline, the happier the client is likely to be.

2. Performance Trigger: Recommended

Of all of the possible crediting methods, none are simpler than the performance trigger method. Here is how it works: If the underlying index is either unchanged or goes up, the client will earn the stated rate of interest. It does not matter how much the index increases. It simply has to stay above the level it reached at the beginning of the crediting period. As an example, let's assume the Performance Trigger rate is four percent and the S&P 500 is at 1500 on the date of issue. As long as the S&P 500 is at 1500 or better one year later, the policyholder will earn four percent.

Typically, the declared Performance rate will be a bit less than declared caps on the annual point-to-point method. This is because the insurance company must pay this full rate even in years when the market return is less than this rate (but is not negative relative to the selected index). The Performance Trigger method will provide better returns than the annual point-to-point in years where the market is just slightly positive, but because the declared trigger rate will be less than the annual caps offered by the point-to-point method, it will earn a bit less in year's where the market does well. However, because every crediting method is working with the same budget with which to purchase the index options, in the long run, these two recommended methods are likely to provide similar returns.

This method obviously has the advantage of being easy to both explain and understand. It's impossible to overstate the importance of meeting the policyholder's earnings expectations when selling indexed annuities. The more the policyholder understands how interest is credited, the more you are likely to meet his or her expectations.

3. Participation Rate: Recommended

The participation rate method is similar to the capped method listed above. The only difference is that rather than applying a cap to the index return, the insurance company credits a percentage of the change in the price of the index. Back when index annuities were first introduced and interest rates were much higher, those percentages were often 100 percent or more. However, in today's interest rate environment, the participation rates will generally be closer to forty to fifty percent. In fact, the point-to-point with a cap method was introduced in response to the need to drop participation rates as interest rates declined. Advisors had grown accustomed to products that captured most, if not all, of the index return. Back then, indexed annuities could indeed be an equity alternative. In fact, that is how they were typically sold in the 1990's. As participation rates declined, advisors (correctly) no longer perceived the product to be an equity alternative. Rather than pivoting and marketing the product as the fixed income alternative that it is today; insurance companies introduced the cap so that they could continue to claim that you got "100% of the index…up to the cap" of the stated percentage.

The beauty of the participation rate method is that it is extremely simple to explain. What client wouldn't understand an explanation of "you will get fifty percent of the change in the S&P 500 index"?

4. "Uncapped" Strategies: Recommended, but with Extreme Caution!

As a result of the outstanding equity performance since 2009, "uncapped" strategies have become increasingly popular. Who wouldn't want to capture more of the market's upside in bull markets? If you ever find yourself thinking that this method is somehow superior in the long run, however, refer back to the chart, 'Indexed Annuity Premium Allocation'. No insurance company is going to be able to buy more options simply because they are offering an uncapped strategy rather than one of the previous 2 methods. Uncapped strategies are typically an annual point-to-point.

For the record, I hate the term "uncapped". At best, it implies that this crediting method will provide superior returns compared with other crediting methods. At worst, it implies that the potential return is unlimited. Neither is true.

Rather than capping the crediting rate, this strategy will limit the possible return in two ways:

1. The underlying index will contain a heavy fixed income component or be managed for volatility, or both. As an example, the actual index could be a composite of an equity index such as the S&P 500 and a fixed income index such as one based on 10-year Treasuries. In addition, asset managers may adjust the allocation between these indices in response to stock market volatility. As an alternative, perhaps only fifty to seventy percent of the underlying return is derived by the return of an actual equity index. The other thirty to fifty percent would

be calculated based on a declared fixed rate that can be as low as one percent.

2. A "spread" is deducted from the "index" return to calculate the final rate credited on the policy. This spread is essentially a deduction from any positive change in the underlying index.

This method is usually calculated annually, which technically makes it a point-to-point crediting method; nevertheless, it can be of any length. You will often see it described as an annual point-to-point with a spread or an uncapped annual point-to-point.

I've probably confused you! Fortunately, I have created an example to help you understand how this method might work.

Example:

The underlying index is an index that is composed of the S&P 500 index and a U.S. Bond Index. The actual weighting can change from day to day based on market volatility. The declared spread is four percent.

The S&P 500 earns twenty percent and the U.S. Bond index earns three percent. To simplify the example, we will assume that the mix between the two indexes is 50/50 (but remember it can change daily).

Credited rate:

S&P return of 20% x .50 = 10%

U.S. Bond index return of 3% x .50 = 1.5%

Total return = 11.5% - 4% spread = 7.5%

You can see that the actual credited rate can, and likely will, differ greatly from the return of the S&P 500. In addition, this method is far more likely than either the annual point-to-point with a cap or the performance trigger methods to generate a zero percent return in a given year. For example, if the S&P 500 returned two percent rather than twenty percent, then the combined return of the two indices would be 2.5 percent. Subtract the four percent spread and you get a negative 1.5 percent. However, since no index annuity can credit a negative return, the policyholder would earn zero percent. Since the annual point-to-point with a cap is based solely on the S&P 500, it would credit two percent in such a year. The Performance Trigger method would return the full-declared trigger rate.

The takeaway on all of this is that the uncapped method will likely provide additional interest in years of strong equity performance. In addition, the pricing actuaries will claim that since the stock market is more likely to earn ten percent or more in a given year than it is zero to ten percent, this method allows the policyholder to benefit from this volatility and therefore should earn one to 1.5 percent more per year on average in the long run. However, this is purely theoretical at this point, so time will tell.

What is absolutely certain is that this method will provide a much greater range of actual earnings from year to year and it will have far more years where no interest is earned. In addition, it is obviously far more difficult to both explain and understand. Therefore, if you select an uncapped strategy, be prepared to answer the question, "why did I get what I got?" far more often than if you select the other strategies. I leave it to you to decide if the extra complexity is worth the potential extra one to 1.5 percent more per year on average in the long run – and I stress the word "potential".

5. Monthly Averaging – Not Recommended

This crediting method takes the average of the underlying index each month during the policy year. The insurance company then either applies a cap or a percentage participation rate on this averaged value. An example will probably help you make sense of this strategy.

Let's assume that a policy is issued on February 1st and it uses the S&P 500 as the underlying index. Let's further assume that the S&P has the following values on the 1st day of the next 12 months:

March 1: 1,000
April 1: 1,010
May 1: 1,040
June 1: 1,020
July 1: 1,050
August 1: 995
September 1: 1,025
October 1: 1,050
November 1: 1,060
December 1: 1,030
January 1: 1,035
February 1: 1,100

Next, we add these 12 values and then divide that total by 12 in order to get the average for the year. That would give you 1,034.58, or a 3.458% increase. This method will then have either a cap or a participation rate applied. Should the cap rate be five percent, then in this example, the policyholder would get the full 3.458 percent. Had the averaged return been 5.5 percent, then the policyholder would only get five percent. If on the other hand, this method comes with a 50 percent participation rate, then the 3.458 percent return would be multiplied by .50, thereby giving the policyholder a final return of 1.729 percent.

It should be readily obvious as to why I do not recommend this method. Firstly, as you can tell, the workings of this crediting method can be difficult to explain and understand. Second, the averaging of the index throughout the year will almost always mute the actual return of the index. In the above example, the index increased 10 percent for the year, but the averaged rate was only 3.458 percent. This occurs because the final index price carries no more weight than every other month. Therefore, the lower values during the earlier months drag down the final return. The only way this will not occur is if the index increases significantly in the early months and then declines through the end of the year. For example, if the value went from 1,000 on March 1 to 1,200 on April 1, only to drop throughout the year down to 1,100 on February 1, then the monthly averaging part of the calculation would actually be greater than the actual index return. But how often will that happen? And even if it does, the cap and or participation rate will still be applied.

The bottom line is that this method is likely to frequently produce results that, at best, will leave the policyholder scratching his or head. At worst, they will fall well short of his or her expectations.

6. Monthly Point to Point with a Cap – Avoid this Method Like the Plague!

If you see an index annuity advertisement (or worse yet, client literature) that claims your client can earn up to 24 percent (or higher), you have stumbled across the monthly point-to-point with a cap method. No interest rate crediting method is more overhyped than this one. If this method is offering a two percent monthly cap, then the policyholder can indeed earn 24 percent in one year with this method. All that has to happen for this "potential" return to become reality is that the market must go up by two percent or more each and every month for a year. I will leave it up to you to conclude how realistic this is.

This method works just like the annual point-to-point (method #1 above), but with one very notable exception: The cap is only applied on the upside, not the downside. Rather than look at the index value at year's end, the insurance company captures the value each month just like the monthly averaging. However, rather than average the values, it sums the changes from one month to the next. Anytime the index is positive from month to month, a cap is applied (typically 1.5-3.0 percent) in order to smooth out the increases. However, typically, no such cap is applied to any down months. This can actually lead to a negative return even if the market goes up. Again, an example will probably help. For this example,

I will assume a monthly cap of two percent on the S&P 500 index is applied on a policy issued on February 1st.

February 1: 1,000

March 1: 1,020 for a change of +2 percent

April 1: 1010 for a change of -0.98 percent

May 1: 1040 for a change of +2.97 percent, therefore, the 2.0 percent cap is applied

June 1: 990 for a change of -4.81 percent

July 1: 1050 for a change of +6.06 percent, therefore, the 2.0 percent cap is applied

August 1: 1035 for a change of -1.42 percent

September 1: 1025 for a change of -0.967 percent

October 1: 1050 for a change of +2.44 percent, therefore, the 2.0 percent cap is applied

November 1: 1060 for a change of +0.952 percent

December 1: 1090 for a change of +2.83 percent, therefore the 2.0 percent cap is applied

January 1: 1120 for a change of +2.75 percent, therefore the 2.0 percent cap is applied

February 1: 1140 for a change of +1.78 percent

The insurance company would then add all of these monthly changes – including the negative ones. This would result in a return of 6.555 percent, on an index that increased 14 percent over the year. Of all of the crediting methods, this will be by far the most volatile and is likely to have the least correlation to the actual market returns. In years where the market moves up and down throughout the year, the return is likely to be close to zero percent or even negative (which would result in no interest credited during the year). On the other hand, if you have a year where the market goes steadily up, this will easily be the best performing method. In fact, this occurred in both 2006 and 2013 – two years where the market went up virtually every month. In such years, this method will provide impressive returns, but you have to ask yourself how likely is it that such a market environment will be duplicated?

Aside from the potential to create unrealistic return expectations, the problems with this crediting method should be obvious. First, good luck getting any client to understand it. My guess is that you probably had to read the above example at least twice just to get a handle on it yourself. I wish you even more luck at answering the question as to how the interest was determined at year-end – especially in years where there is little correlation to the market. You will need to capture the index value on each monthly policy anniversary for each of your clients and then calculate their individual returns. Due to timing differences, two people who purchase policies with this crediting method just a few days apart can experience very different results.

Because of the variability in annual returns, you should expect clients to ask, "How did I get this return?" virtually every year. And finally, if you have two to three very poor months during the year, the fact that these months won't be capped while the up months will be, could easily lead to virtually no interest credited even if the market went up 10 percent or more. In my view, the potential for this method to credit little or no interest even in a year when the underlying index goes up 10 percent or more should be more than enough reason to avoid this crediting method.

Commonly Used Indexes

If you only picked up one thing from this chapter, it should be to keep things simple. Ever since insurance companies introduced indexed annuities, they have made the S&P 500 the most prominent index choice against which to benchmark returns. In my opinion, this is a good thing. Using a universally recognizable, easy to track index greatly simplifies the indexed annuity story. Today, however, you will find products that offer returns based on many index choices – everything from the Dow Jones Industrial Average to the Russell 2000 to the MSCI EAFE. Some products will credit interest based on the positive return on Treasury Bonds. If you think interest rates are going to rise, then you can select a crediting method that is based on an inverse Treasury bond index.

In recent years, insurance companies have been introducing volatility-managed indices. For example, one major index annuity company uses the Barclays US Dynamic Balance index. You will typically find these indexes used with uncapped interest crediting strategies. Given the downside protection provided by index annuities, it is not realistic to expect to earn the full market return on the upside. If that were possible, we could all put all of our money into indexed annuities and never have to worry again. The upside has to be limited in some way. If it's not done with a hard cap on earnings, then the underlying index must provide the limits. For example, the Barclays US Dynamic Balance Index is comprised of the Barclays Capital U.S. Aggregate Bond Index and the S&P 500 Index. The weighting between these two indices can shift as often as daily based on current market volatility.

Does It Matter Which Index I Use?

The current selection of indices offers such similar returns that, in my opinion it doesn't matter which index you direct the client to use. No matter which index you choose, the same amount of money is available to purchase the options on the index. If one particular index has a higher expected return than another, then the options on that index will cost more, therefore the insurance company will be able to purchase fewer option contracts. In other words, the long-term expected return from the options should always be very similar.

I recommend just sticking with the S&P 500. Why spend extra time explaining an index that the policyholder has never ever heard of – especially if that particular index can't easily be tracked in the paper or online?

Should I Use Multiple Indices On One Policy?

Returns will vary each year from index to index; so, one prevalent method of diversifying returns is to select multiple indices. This approach will lower the likelihood that the policyholder will earn zero percent in any given year. If you use two, three or even four different indexes, then in years of modest market declines, it likely that at least one of them will provide a positive return. Obviously, avoiding years of zero percent interest is attractive to policyholders. However, this method will also limit the upside. Essentially, a multiple index strategy will smooth out the expected earnings and provide the policyholder with returns that more consistently match the long-term expected returns of regular fixed annuities.

I would caution you against too much diversification. If you select multiple indices along with multiple interest crediting strategies, you will likely dilute the returns down to the point that you have essentially turned the index annuity into a traditional fixed annuity.

The Minimum-Rate Guarantee – A Misunderstood Concept

All indexed annuities must provide a minimum guaranteed rate before regulators will classify them as fixed annuities and not securities. This rate comes in a variety of styles. It could be expressed as a percentage on part of the premium (i.e., three percent on 87.5 percent of the premium) or a percentage on all of the premium (i.e., one percent on 100 percent of the premium). The minimum guarantee is designed to provide an assurance that the policyholder will be entitled to a return of premium at some date in the future, even if the selected index crediting option(s) somehow provide no return year after year.

It is a common misconception that this minimum rate is the least amount of interest credited each year. That is simply not the case. The insurance company calculates two separate values on the policy – the value determined by the selected interest crediting strategy and the value calculated by the minimum rate. When the policy is cashed in, the policyholder gets the greater of these two values. The reality is that the minimum rate value will rarely come into play – especially if it's calculated on just a portion of the premium. A simple example will show why this is the case. In this example, we will assume that the minimum value is one percent on 100 percent of the $100,000 premium. We will also assume that the cap on the S&P 500 index is five percent each year.

Contract Year	Min. rate of 1%	Min. Account Value	S&P 500 Change	Earned rate on Interest Credited Strategy	Account Value
1	1%	$101,000	10%	5%	$105,000
2	1%	$102,010	3%	3%	$108,150
3	1%	$103,030	-10%	0%	$108,150
4	1%	$104,060	15%	5%	$113,557
5	1%	$105,101	-15%	0%	$113,557

Two things are readily apparent in this example. First, the policyholder did not get one percent added to the account in the two years where the market goes down. As mentioned previously, this one percent only applies to the minimum contract value. The policyholder does not get the greater of the two returns each year. Second, the minimum value becomes irrelevant very quickly. No drop in the underlying index ever causes the account value to drop from year to year. The effect is that the policyholder locks in the gains, if any, each year. In the above example, the account value reaches $108,150 by the end of the 2nd year. The minimum value won't surpass this amount until year eight. The S&P 500 would have to be flat or down for six consecutive years for the minimum account value to be used as the actual value. The bottom line is that once an indexed policy earns the cap in a given year, the minimum guaranteed value effectively becomes meaningless from that point forward.

The Importance of the Annual Reset

At this point, toward the end of the chapter, you might wonder why I waited until now to discuss the annual reset feature. I would argue that the annual reset feature is perhaps the single most important feature that makes an indexed annuity worth consideration in a client's portfolio. However, its importance is more readily understood once you understand how the product itself is structured.

The annual reset feature allows the policyholder to have interest credited to the account value in every year that the underlying index is up. Because the insurance company "resets" the index price on each policy anniversary, the policyholder does not have to wait until the index recovers in order to earn interest in a year after a down year. Let's again use an example of a $100,000 policy based on the S&P 500 with a five percent cap.

Contract Year	S&P 500 Value	S&P 500 Change	Earned rate on Interest Credited Strategy	Account Value
0	1,500	NA	NA	$100,000
1	1,600	6.67%	5%	$105,000
2	1,750	16.04%	5%	$110,250
3	1,400	-25.00%	0%	$110,250
4	1,450	3.57%	3.57%	$114,186

Notice that after four years, the S&P 500 is actually below the starting value. Despite that, the policyholder earned interest in year four. This is because the starting point for year four is the 1,400 value at the end of year three. Each year, the insurance company "resets" the starting index value for the next year based on the current value. Just think how great it would be if we could do that with all of our investments.

Potential Index Annuity Clients

One principle bears repeating: an indexed annuity is not an alternative to equities. If you can keep this in mind, then you are well on your way to using this product appropriately. The following four situations will cover 95 percent of all of the reasons that an indexed annuity is a suitable option for a client's portfolio:

1. The CD buyer that wants to earn more than the bank is willing to pay

One of the most obvious potential indexed annuity client is one who would buy a certificate of deposit. This type of client wants to know that his or her money is safe. Return *of* their money is far more important than the return *on* their money. Nevertheless, they would like to earn more than what is available in today's world of low interest rates. *If the client is willing to give up the guaranteed rate of return each year*, and trade that for an unknown annual return – one that is likely to be zero percent, but never negative about 20 percent to 25 percent of the time – then an index annuity is a good alternative. Over the long run, an indexed annuity is likely to provide returns that are about two - three percent per year more than bank CDs with a maturity of five years or less. However, it's very important that you make sure the client understands that while indexed annuities are very safe, they are not FDIC insured. If the client needs that insurance in order to sleep well at night, an indexed annuity is not suitable for his or her needs.

2. The fixed annuity buyer who wants more return

Occasionally you will encounter clients who want to see a satisfactory yield on his or her money. Indeed, I am tempted make this reason 1a) because it follows the same rationale that drives the CD buyer. In my view, the only traditional fixed annuities that should be offered today are multi-year rate guarantee products. If the client wants to know exactly how much he or she will earn during the length of the surrender charge period, then a fixed annuity that offers a guaranteed rate through the surrender charge period will be the better choice. Why not look at a traditional fixed annuity that declares a rate one year at a time? With a traditional fixed annuity, the policyholder does not know what interest she will earn each year. The only thing she knows is that she will earn at least the minimum rate. If she is OK with getting a varying return each year, then show her an indexed annuity as an alternative.

3. The fixed income client that buys bonds primarily for principal protection

A significant number of fixed-income investors buy bonds mostly to diversify and reduce the volatility of their overall portfolio. For these clients, the income is just a bonus. They have been trained to keep a 50/50 or 60/40 balance of equities and bonds. However, with 10-year Treasuries below three percent, they are concerned (or you are concerned for them) that bonds will not serve this purpose if interest rates rise. After almost 40 years of declining interest rates, they have become used to using bonds as a safe haven. But what happens when bond prices start heading the other way? How will they fund that 40 to 50 percent of the portfolio? In addition, given the market rally since 2009, many portfolios are too heavily weighted into equities. Rather than reallocate some of the equity portion solely to bonds, I would suggest using index annuities as part of the 40 to 50 percent. Over the long run, index returns should be equivalent to investment-grade bonds, but without the interest rate risk.

4. An alternative to a deferred income annuity or a variable annuity with a living benefit

If the goal is to provide a future known income stream with the least amount of capital, an indexed annuity with a living benefit is likely to be the answer. I cover this in detail in the chapter on living benefits, so I'll keep it short here. The insurance company does not have to worry about the index annuity falling, so they will always be able to provide more initial guaranteed income with an indexed annuity than with a variable annuity. In the long run, market step-ups could cause the variable annuity to provide more income, but this will never be the case at the time of purchase. One would think that since a deferred income annuity has far less liquidity than an indexed annuity, it would always guarantee more future income than an indexed annuity with a living benefit. However, this is often not the case. On a deferred income annuity, the insurance company must assume that only the policyholders that die prior to the income date will not receive the guaranteed amount of income. On an indexed annuity, they can assume that a certain percentage of the policies will lapse prior to the income date. Lapsed policies allow insurance companies to collect living benefit fees on a benefit that essentially goes unused. Insurance companies therefore use this extra fee income as a means to increase the guaranteed income under the rider.

Before you offer a deferred income annuity to any of your clients, always check to see if an indexed annuity with a living benefit will provide more guaranteed income to go along with the greater liquidity.

Common Objections to Index Annuities

1. Commissions and surrender charges are too high

The biggest criticism of all annuities is that the commissions are too high and therefore the surrender charges which help support the commissions are too high as well. Often, the drawbacks of annuities come down to factors that have the potential to diminish policyholder benefits. Sadly, this sometimes is true. Fortunately, it is becoming less true all of the time. When indexed annuities began to gain popularity after the Dotcom Crash of 2000 to 2002, far too many insurance companies designed products that were more concerned about benefiting the selling agent rather than the policyholder. Commissions in excess of 10 percent were not uncommon. Throw in one to two percent in commission for the Independent Marketing Organization that was distributing the product, and it's not hard to see how there would be little left over to pay reasonable returns to the policyholder. And if the insurance company is going to front a commission of 10 percent or more out of its pocket, it has to protect itself with surrender charges in excess of 10 percent that will run 15 years or more. But there have always been consumer friendly designed indexed annuities, and there are more and more all of the time. Look for indexed annuities with surrender charge periods of seven years or less, and you will likely have one that offers good consumer value. Why focus on the surrender charge period? Because the length and amount of the surrender charge is driven by the commission schedule. The lower the commission, the lower the surrender charge and consequently, the more money available to pay interest to the policyholder. I will also note that a longer surrender charge is not necessarily a negative strike on these instruments. In addition to allowing the insurance company to recover the commissions if the policy is cashed out early, the longer surrender charge also can allow the insurance company to price the product with a lower lapse assumption and a lower reserve requirement. This allows them to assume that the policy will be in effect longer, thereby allowing the insurance company to allocate more money to the options piece of the pricing pie, which in turn allows the company to offer higher cap rates.

2. Index Annuities are Too Complex

They can be. A contract with multiple interest crediting strategies on multiple indices can be difficult to sort out. Throw in a living benefit and you need a 20-page brochure just to explain the product! If you have gotten nothing else out of this chapter, remember that simplicity should always be your guide. One index with one crediting strategy is all you need. I recommend the S&P 500 index with the annual point to point, but as long as you can answer the question, "how did they calculate my interest for this year?" any index with either a point to point or a performance trigger method will work.

3. But what if the index goes down five years in a row?

Remember when I said clients believe that return *of* their money is far more important than return *on* their money. People don't mind getting zero percent occasionally, but they hate the thought of getting 0% frequently. If you understand the importance of the annual reset feature, you will realize how unlikely it is that the policyholder will earn no interest on a frequent basis. The fact of the matter is that the stock market rarely goes down multiple years in a row. Even during 2007-09, if you look at the return of the S&P 500 on a calendar basis, you will see that the market actually went up in both 2007 and 2009 (thirty years from now, people are likely to look at the annual market performance of 2007-09 and wonder what the big deal was). Statistics show that a policyholder that chooses an annual reset crediting method will earn the cap rate (at today's rates) about 60 percent of the time, will earn between zero percent and the cap rate, fifteen to twenty percent of the time and will earn zero percent about twenty to twenty-five percent of the time.

I will note however, that these percentages could be significantly different under the uncapped strategies that are now becoming popular. Uncapped strategies will have a greater range of possible returns. The spread (or fee) that is deducted from the calculated return makes it far more likely that the final crediting rate will be zero percent. This is the trade-off for the potential for higher returns in the years the market does well.

4. The insurance company can change the caps and spreads from year to year

This is a very real concern. Insurance companies do have the ability to change the caps and spreads, from year to year and will adjust them in line with the options they buy to provide the actual returns. They may also change the caps and spreads if they realize they mispriced the products initially. However, the insurance companies also understand that if they want to hold or gain market share, they must maintain the competitiveness of the product even after it is issued. Before you start selling an indexed annuity for a particular carrier, ask for a history of its renewal rates. If they will not or cannot provide it, look for another company. I would also suggest that you offer products only from insurance companies that have a track record of committing to the annuity industry. Once a company elects to cease distributing annuities through 3rd parties such as banks and broker-dealers, their incentive to keep caps and spreads competitive greatly diminishes.

5. The caps for indexed annuities are too low compared to the potential return of the stock market

If you hear this objection, it means the client (or advisor) is looking at an indexed annuity as an equity alternative. It is not. If the market goes up twenty percent, do you get mad because your bonds, bond fund or CD only returned four percent? Of course not, because you know that's not what those products are designed to do. An index annuity is no different. It's not designed to be a substitute for equity money. It's designed to be a substitute for principal protected money. It just happens to have a return that is tied to the stock market.

Key Takeaway

I am unable to adequately express the importance of keeping index choices uncomplicated, so I will leave it to Leonardo da Vinci, the polymath of the Italian Renaissance.

"Simplicity is the ultimate sophistication."

Find one or two index strategies you like and can easily explain to your clients and select the S&P 500 as your underlying index. Set your client's expectations appropriately. In the long run, an indexed annuity should credit one to two percent more per year than a fixed annuity, and three to four percent more per year than a one year Certificate of Deposit. Never lead the policyholder to believe that an indexed annuity is designed to provide returns that are similar to equities. Yes, the returns are ultimately determined by a stock index, but this index is nothing more than a scoring mechanism. The policyholder is never invested in that underlying index and will never earn returns matching that index in the long run. Make sure the policyholder understands that he or she will earn zero percent about twenty percent of the time, will earn the cap rate about 55 percent of the time and will earn something in between in all other years. As long as you properly manage expectations and are able to answer the question, "why did I get what I got?" you will find your indexed annuity clients to be amongst your most satisfied clients.

CHAPTER 3

IMMEDIATE ANNUITIES – OVERLOOKED & UNDERRATED

Almost everyone wants a pension – especially those that don't have one. Despite this, only about $10 billion in immediate annuities, a product that could be described as a self-funded pension, are purchased each year[i]. For over two decades now the insurance industry has expected a great surge in immediate annuity sales, mostly to the just under 77 million baby boomers who began turning 65 in 2011[ii]. The popular theory was that they would insist on a guaranteed lifetime income, and the insurance industry stood ready to oblige. Yet here we are in 2019, eight years after the first baby boomer reached the age of 65 and the tidal wave has been little more than a trickle. While immediate annuity sales have indeed increased, at most broker/dealers they still make up less than five percent of all annuity sales. It is a shame really, because immediate annuities provide something that few, if any, other investments can – a check that will arrive in the policyholder's mailbox every month for as long as her or she (or both) live. Any immediate annuity policyholder will tell you that there is something very reassuring in knowing that the income will continue no matter what happens to the stock market, to interest rates or to public policies in Washington DC.

What is an immediate annuity?

Ann immediate annuity is a lump sum given to an insurance company in exchange for a regular income for a specified amount of time. The concept is hardly new. The insurance industry has been issuing annuities for decades, although the early contracts were usually based on periodic premiums paid by the insured for a number of years rather than a lump sum. The ad below appeared in a 1966 issue of Life Magazine. Given that my copy is a copy of a copy of a copy, thereby making the text difficult to read, I have transcribed the text below.

"How we retired in 15 years with $300 a month"
Life Magazine ad January 21, 1966

"Look at us! We're retired and having the time of our lives ...Let me tell you about it.

I started thinking about retiring in 1950. Nancy thought I was silly. It all seemed so far away. "And besides," she said, "It makes me feel old". It didn't seem silly to me though. We had just spent the afternoon with Nancy's aunt and uncle. Uncle Will had turned 45 during the war, and by 1945 his working days were over.

Now life seemed to be standing still for them. They couldn't even take the short weekend trips their friends could afford. They couldn't visit their children as often as they liked. A pretty grim existence, I thought. But why? He'd had a great job. Then Nancy reminded me- they had never planned ahead. During her uncle's working years, his paycheck was spent almost as soon as it arrived. Fortunately, they had put some money away for a rainy day, but they hadn't planned ahead enough to make those retirement days sunny.

Not for me, I decided. When it's time for us to retire, I want to be able to do the things we always dreamed of doing instead of counting every penny. I showed Nancy a _____ insurance company ad I saw in Life Magazine a week or so before. It described their retirement income plan, telling how a man of 40 could retire in 15 years with a guaranteed income of $300 or more for life. Nancy agreed it was a great plan. The thought of retiring at 55 didn't make her feel old at all! So I filled in the coupon that day and sent it right off.

A few days later, the booklet describing the _____ insurance company plan arrived. I picked the right one for us and signed up right away. Three months ago, my first check arrived – right on time.

Last month we moved down here to Florida, and we love it.
Nancy looks great with her tan, and she's thrilled at the
thought of keeping it all year long! My tan suits me fine, but
I'm really hooked on the fish. Whether I catch one a day or
seven (or more), I'm having the time of my life, because we
saved for a rainy day with _____ insurance company.
Send for a free booklet

This story is typical. Assuming you start early enough, you
can plan to have an income of from $50 to $500 a month or
more beginning at age 55, 60, 65 or older. Send the coupon
and receive by mail, without charge or obligation, a booklet
that tells about _____ insurance company plans. Similar plans
are available for women – and for Employee Pension
Programs. Send for your free copy now. In 15 years, you'll be
glad you did.

I can't help but chuckle every time I read this ad. As if the corny
references to retiring to Florida aren't enough, the thought of being
happy about living the good life on $300 per month just boggles my
mind. The ad shows the happy, smiling couple sitting in a small fishing
boat, holding up a fish the just caught. I can't help but think,
facetiously, that the couple in the ad is smiling because they
successfully caught their dinner for the evening rather than because
they are having the time of their life. And retiring at 55? Three hundred
dollars might have been able to cover substantially more in monthly
living expenses than it can today, but that amount would still have to

44

sustain them for almost 40 years of retirement based on today's expectations of longevity.

As dated as it is, this ad still portrays both the good and the bad aspects of an immediate annuity. It does indeed give you a monthly check for life, but it also must be large enough to outpace years of inflation.

The ad is remarkable for another reason: People still want the same things out of retirement now that they did in 1966. People still want the assurance of a steady retirement check that they cannot outlive. Change the retirement age to 65 rather than 55 and update the income amount by a factor of ten and this ad could describe an important financial goal of many of today's baby boomers.

Types of Immediate Annuities

A common criticism of immediate annuities is the belief, misguided in my opinion, that payouts stop as soon as you die. Clients seem to have this concern that the excitement of receiving their first check will induce a heart attack and cause them to drop dead, thereby allowing the insurance company to keep the balance of the investment. Such a statement would be true only if the policyholder purchased a life-only annuity, and that is an option almost no one chooses. In fact, a life-only annuity would make sense only if the policyholder has no heirs that need income upon his or her death (including a spouse) and the goal is to receive the largest possible income check with the least amount of money. Even under those circumstances, few would be willing to buy a life-only annuity for fear of "losing to the insurance company." With that in mind, I will describe the more popular and suitable immediate annuity options.

To understand how the various options, affect the income payments, you need to understand two concepts. First, the greater the contingent guarantees, the lower the income payment. This is why the life–only annuity option always pays the most money. The insurance company is basing the payments on a single life with no other contingent guarantees. Second, the older the individual upon whom the income is based (the annuitant), the higher the payments. The reason for this should be obvious: The older you are the lower your life expectancy, therefore the shorter the length of time the insurance company expects to have to make payments.

1. Joint & Survivor – Pays an income based on two lives. Upon the death of the first individual, the payments will continue at either 100 percent of the original income or a smaller percentage such as 67 percent (under the assumption that one can live more cheaply than two). This is a common choice for spouses. The benefit of choosing a reduced income percentage upon the first death is a higher initial income since the insurance company is on the hook for a lower payment upon the first death.

2. Cash Refund – Should the individual(s) receiving the payments die before the total income payments equal the initial amount invested, the insurance company will pay the beneficiary the difference in a lump sum. This is a popular option because the policyholder knows that the insurance company cannot pay out less than the amount originally invested. This option overcomes the concern that the insurance company will "win" if the policyholder does not live to his or her life expectancy.

3. Installment Refund – Very similar to the cash refund, except the insurance company continues to pay the income payments to the beneficiary until the amount originally invested is paid out. Once that occurs, the income payments stop.

4. Life and Term Certain – This option pays income payments for the greater of the life of the annuitant or the length of the term-certain period, typically 10 or 20 years. If the annuitant dies prior to the term-certain period, payments will be made to the beneficiary until the term certain period ends.

These various options can impact the income amounts differently. Take a look below at the side-by-side comparisons of income would be paid out to a 65-year-old and 75-year-old, both of whom invested $100,000, in immediate annuities.

Payout Option	Age 65	Age 75
Life Only – Male	$542 (76% tax free)	$739 (90% tax free)
Life & 10 Years – Male	$540 (74% tax free)	$699 (82% tax free)
Life & 20 Years – Male	$494 (69% tax free)	$549 (73% tax free)
Joint & Survivor 100% (Male & Female)	$459 (73% tax free)	$584 (87% tax free)
Cash Refund – Male	$505 (72% tax free)	$629 (80% tax free)
Installment Refund – Male	$513 (71% tax free)	$656 (73% tax free)

All of the above calculations assume a policy issued in Florida as of 5/1/19.

You can see how the income drops as the guarantees go up. There is only a slight drop in income between the life only and the life and 10 years certain option for the 65-year-old, because it is highly likely the owner will live to at least 75. Therefore, the additional guarantee by the insurance company is not that costly. However, once you go to life and 20 years certain, you see a significant drop in income. The life expectancy of a 65-year-old male is less than 20 years, therefore guaranteeing the income for 20 years has significant cost.

You can also see the big increase in income for the 75-year old. This is obviously due to the shorter life expectancy. The older the policyholder is, the more the income is driven by the policyholder's life expectancy and the less it's driven by interest rates (more on that later). This makes immediate annuities a particularly attractive alternative to older individuals.

Should I buy a COLA immediate annuity?

Any of the above annuity options can also be purchased with an increasing annual payment of a specified percentage, typically three percent. On the surface, this option seems to make complete sense, and it would significantly boost income for the couple in the Life Magazine ad, who would not have to rely on just $300 per month for the rest of their lives – even if the dollar's buying power was stronger in the late 1960s than it is now. In my opinion, this option is simply not worth the cost. Obviously, if the insurance company promises to increase the income payment each year, it is going to give the policyholder less money initially. For example, if the 65-year-old couple in the above example elected to take a cash refund option with a three percent annual increase, they would only receive $310 per month, rather than the $459 per month without the annual increase. With the income increasing three percent per year, it will be year 13 before they reach the amount of income, they would have had in the first year had they not chosen the annual increase. At that point, they would both be 78 years old. Rather than purchase a COLA on the annuity, utilize the rest of the portfolio to generate future income needs. For example, this particular couple would have to put 48% more into a 3% COLA annuity to get the same initial income as the annuity without the COLA. Rather than put the extra money in the annuity, I would suggest they use those funds to buy either a mutual fund or variable annuity. They can then use that money to provide additional income in later years – either by making systematic withdrawals or using the money to buy additional immediate annuities every five or 10 years.

What is the internal return on an immediate annuity?

At this stage in discussions about immediate annuities you might be asking, 'Wait, how should I calculate the internal rate of return on an immediate annuity?' That is not surprising, because financial advisors have been trained to think in terms of rates of returns on every investment they recommend. Immediate annuities can only be quoted in terms of cash flow, not yield. You simply cannot accurately compare the cash flow of an annuity with the yield on other fixed income investments. Therefore, the actual rate of return cannot be calculated until after the annuitant dies. Tell me the date the annuitant (or joint annuitants) is expected to pass away, and only then will I be able to calculate the precise rate of return. The truth is that unless you have some kind of divine insight into your clients' mortality, the best that I – or anyone – can do is give you an expected rate of return. As a rule of thumb, insurance companies price immediate annuities to return 10-year Treasuries plus 0.5 – 1.0 percent over an individual's life expectancy. Obviously, no one is going to get excited about this expected return, but immediate annuities are not about a rate of return. They are about insuring against the risk a client you will outlive his or her money. No one asks about a rate of return before buying auto insurance, homeowner's insurance or long–term care insurance. They are paying a known cost (the premium) in order to avoid a potential future liability. In that sense, immediate annuities provide peace of mind. They allow the policyholder to sleep well knowing that a known amount of money will arrive each month even if that policyholder lives to 120.

Quote Cash Flow, Not a Rate of Return

Far too often people quote the annual cash flow created by an immediate annuity as the rate of return. My introduction quoted the 1944 "Modern Business" book series that I found on the shelves of a vacation house my family recently rented. Among the furnishings was a series of old books on the living room bookshelf. One book in this series was simply titled "Insurance." The author laid out a scenario of a $1,000 annuity that pays $69.66 per year, and they state that the "apparent rate of return for the money invested is 6.966 per cent," thereby giving us evidence that immediate annuity returns have been commonly misquoted for decades. As I stated earlier, unless you know exactly when the annuitant will die, calculating the actual yield on the investments. But don't make the same mistake as the author of the Modern Business Series, and countless others since their book was published. Make sure your clients understand that the income generated from the immediate annuity is a cash flow that is made up of both principal and interest. It is not a current yield.

Common Objections to Immediate Annuities

I will never forget a particular industry meeting that I attended in the early 1990's. I don't remember the exact year, but I do remember that it was the Annual Marketing Conference for the National Association of Variable Annuities (NAVA), the predecessor to the Insured Retirement Institute (IRI). The buzz at the conference was that Dick Austin (who in my opinion is the grandfather of immediate annuities) was going to make the presentation that finally pushed immediate annuities into the mainstream. Sure enough, Dick's session was packed, yet everyone in attendance worked for an insurance company. I didn't see a single broker/dealer representative. It's been almost 30 years since Dick's presentation, but immediate annuity sales still suffer from the same common objections. These include:

1. **Immediate annuities are a terrible investment (the implied rate of return is too low)** – The reality is that while this is a common objection by financial advisors, your clients don't share this objection. As I said previously, for the policyholder, it's about getting a check they can't outlive. Clients don't ask about the rate of return on their pension or social security payment. They just want to know how big the check is. Immediate annuities are no different.

2. **If you die, the insurance company keeps all of your money** - This is true only if the policyholder chooses a life only annuity. Almost no one does.

3. **The client (and the advisor) gives up control of the money** - While there are some immediate annuities that allow the policyholder to commute the future income payments, and immediate annuities can normally be easily sold to outside investors; these options are rarely in the policyholder's best interest. They should be exercised only if the client is in desperate need of liquidity. Therefore, it is true that the policyholder is essentially giving up control of the money in exchange for a stream of income. Essentially, the policyholder is *funding* his or

her own pension in exchange for expert asset management. Why is that such a bad idea? How often does someone ever want to turn his or her pension or social security payments into cash? And yes, you as the advisor do lose control over the percentage of the client's assets that are used to fund the annuity. But think about how much more flexibility you have investing the rest of the client's portfolio when you know the essential expenses are covered by the monthly annuity payment. If you attempt to provide lifetime income through a systematic withdrawal rate of the entire portfolio, you must structure a more conservative, and therefore less volatile portfolio in order to maximize the probability that the client will not run out of money and to minimize the sequence of returns risk. If you utilize an immediate annuity to help cover the essential expenses, you have the flexibility to invest the remaining assets much more aggressively. As an example, think about two clients that ask your advice about how to structure a retirement income portfolio. One client has both a pension and social security and the other client only receives social security. How much easier is it for you to design the portfolio for the client with the pension?

4. Immediate annuities don't keep pace with inflation – It's hard to argue with this objection. Unless you elect an immediate annuity option that increases by a certain percentage each year, the immediate annuity will throw off the same amount of income in year 20 that it did in year one. For the reasons mentioned above, I don't believe that immediate annuities with a rising income are worth the reduction in the initial income. But the reality is, clients don't look for an increase in their retirement incomes each and every year. They typically look to adjust their income every three to five years to match their changing lifestyles. If you have properly structured the client's portfolio (and the client has saved enough), then you should be able to fund these increases from the client's other assets. You might even buy a small immediate annuity to supplement the original one every five years or so.

5. Immediate annuities shouldn't be purchased when interest rates are low – Although I now see frequent articles about the benefits of an immediate annuity, these articles often come with a recommendation to wait until interest rates move back up. Since interest rates help determine the amount of income an immediate annuity will provide you, the basic premise behind the recommendation to wait is that it makes little sense to lock in a lifetime income stream at today's continually low interest rates. However, such advice is typically based on a lack of understanding of how immediate annuities are priced. You see, unlike CD's and bonds – both of which are priced based primarily on interest rates and maturity – a significant portion of the income you will receive from an immediate annuity is based on your life expectancy. In fact, the older you are, the greater the impact of your life expectancy relative to the current level of interest rates. Therefore, as interest rates have come down over the last 30 years, the amount of income paid on newly purchased immediate annuities has declined significantly less than other low risk investments that are often used for retirement income.

Example: Male age 65, needing $30,000/ year income - Cash Refund Option

In 2005, you would have had to put $775,194 into a 5-year certificate of deposit at the then average rate of 3.9% to generate $30,000 a year. Just seven years later, due to historically low interest rates, it would take over $3 million to generate that same $30,000 in income. By comparison, in 2005, a 65-year-old male would have had to put $420,961 into an immediate annuity to guarantee $30,000 a year for life. That carries the additional promise of the cash refund option, in which the insurance company pays the purchaser's beneficiary a lump sum equal to the difference between the $420,961 and the total payments made, should the purchaser die prematurely. In 2012, due to lower interest rates, it would have indeed taken more money to duplicate that same level of income. However, since a major portion of the pricing of the annuity is based on life expectancy, you would have only needed 25 percent more.

Critics of this argument might be quick to point out that I'm comparing apples to oranges with this example. To an extent, they would be right. The CD is providing the $30,000 in income solely from the interest earned on the CD. When the CD matures in five years, the $3 million would still be intact. This is not the case with the annuity since it is returning your principal and interest to you over your lifetime. Once the annuity has paid out $525,915, the only thing you are entitled to receive is the $30,000 in annual income for as long as you live. However, this criticism assumes that both of these choices are available to you. If you need $30,000 in annual income and you don't have $3 million, you are going to be spending both your principal and interest no matter what approach you take. Therefore, the goal is to generate the income as efficiently as possible. And yes, you could wait until interest rates go back up. When this occurs, you will get more income from the annuity. Plus, you would have the added advantage of being older, thereby giving you more income due to your life expectancy. However, I've heard advisors recommending to their clients that they wait until "interest rates go back up" for 25 years now. Eventually, those suggesting you wait will prove to be right. The only question is can your clients wait that long?

Variable Annuitization

There's probably a good chance that you are saying, "variable annuitization? What's that?" If so, you would not be alone. In my opinion, variable annuitization is the most underutilized aspect of the annuity industry. In fact, when variable annuities are annuitized (which they rarely are), they are typically converted to a fixed annuitization. With a fixed annuitization, as demonstrated in all of the examples above, the annuitant gets a fixed amount of money each month. With a variable annuitization, the annuitant gets a fixed number of sub-account units each month. These units continue to be invested in the same sub-accounts that were used during the accumulation phase of the annuity. As the value of the units goes up and down, the amount of income goes up or down with them. Over time, this option will provide the annuitant with a rising amount of income. In fact, if the annuitant has a long-life expectancy, he or she will undoubtedly receive far more income in retirement than a person that selects a fixed annuitization payout. So why don't more people choose this option? It comes down to three reasons:

1. **Nothing in the annuity business comes without a tradeoff.** Because the insurance company will likely have to increase the income over time, variable annuitization will always pay less income initially than fixed annuitization. Typically, it will start at about 75 percent of what an equivalent fixed annuity will pay.

2. **What goes up can also come down.** Consider someone that was getting income through variable annuitization during the financial crises. Imagine how they would feel if their income fell 30 percent to 50 percent. Of course, it would have quickly recovered and would likely now be providing even more income than before, but most people want a more predictable income stream. Therefore, variable annuitization should never be a client's sole source of income.

3. **Almost no one realizes it is an option.** Why? Because no one, including the insurance companies, have made any effort to promote this option. The consensus is that the amount of sales generated would not be worth the effort. After all, if the industry hasn't been successful getting policyholders to choose a fixed annuitization, what are the odds the industry will have much success getting policyholders to choose an annuity income that fluctuates?

The Mechanics Behind Variable Annuitization

Variable annuitization rates are always quoted with an Assumed Rate of Return (ARR). The ARR is typically three percent to four percent, but it can be higher or lower. This ARR represents that rate of return that must be achieved by the underlying sub-accounts in order for the annuitant to get an increase in income. In other words, if the ARR is four percent, and the sub-accounts return six percent, then the annuitant will see a two percent increase in income. Similarly, if the sub-accounts return two percent, then the annuitant will experience a two percent drop in income. The higher the ARR, the higher the initial income amount. Since the annuitant with a four percent ARR has a higher hurdle than the annuitant with a three percent ARR, the trade-off is that the annuitant with the four percent ARR will receive more income to start.

Taxation of Annuitized Policies

The focus of this section will be only on annuities purchased in a non-qualified plan. If an annuity is annuitized within a qualified plan, it is taxed like any other asset within that plan. Annuities have unique tax implications only if purchased in a non-qualified plan.

Exclusion Allowances for All

All non-qualified annuities are allowed an exclusion allowance when calculating the taxable portion of any annuity payment. This exclusion allowance calculates a percentage of each payment that is considered a return of principal and is therefore non-taxable. This amount is based on the amount of time the insurance company expects to make income payments. For example, if the insurance company expects to make income payments for 20 years, then it will assume that the policyholder will receive $1/20^{th}$ of the principal each year. Obviously, the annuitant's life expectancy is the biggest factor affecting the withdrawal rate, but the additional guarantees are considered as well. If you look back at the table of income calculations for the 65- and 75-year-olds, you can see how the exclusion ratio changes based on the various payment scheme. All else being equal, a 65-year-old will have a lower exclusion ratio than a 75-year-old because the payments are expected to last longer. Similarly, a Life and 20-years-certain payment will have a lower exclusion ratio than a life only payment because the 20-year minimum term will also cause the payments to be longer on average.

If you stop to think about it, virtually no immediate annuity will pay exactly as long as expected. Either the annuitant will die before the 100 percent of the principal is paid out or the annuitant will still be alive after 100 percent of the principal is paid out. So, what happens then? If the payments stop before the entire principal is recovered, then the policyholder essentially has reported too much income during the income period. The policyholder's estate is therefore allowed to take an ordinary loss on the final income tax return filed by the estate. If on the other hand the annuitant is still alive and receiving payments after the entire principal is received, 100 percent of the remaining income payments become taxable each year.

Exclusion Allowance For Variable Annuitization

For fixed immediate annuities, the exclusion allowance is a set percentage of each payment. It never changes until the policyholder receives the entire principal. If the policyholder elects variable annuitization from a variable annuity, it works a bit differently because the income payments change every month. The initial exclusion allowance is calculated in the same manner as fixed annuitization. Once the initial percentage is calculated, however, the insurance company determines how many units at the current unit price are required to create the exclusion allowance. Remember: on variable annuitization, the annuitant receives a fixed number of units each month, not a fixed number of dollars. For all future payments, the exclusion allowance will be that same amount of units. Therefore, while the exclusion allowance will always be a set percentage of the monthly payment, the actual dollar amount of the allowance will go up and down with the unit value of the underlying sub-account(s).

Who Gets The Tax Bill?

This is a critical point: Regardless of who receives the income payments, the policy owner pays any taxes due. In addition, if payments are made to someone other than the owner, the owner is deemed to have made a taxable gift to the recipient of those payments. These rules are clearly designed to keep people from using annuities as an estate-planning tool.

Keep things simple. Ensure that the owner and the annuitant are the same party, (always a good rule for annuities) and name as the beneficiary whoever they want to receive any additional payments when the owner/annuitant dies.

Creditor Protection

In most states, annuitized policies are protected from creditors and are not eligible for seizure in bankruptcies. This obviously makes this an attractive option for certain professionals, such as doctors. I would advise that you check the applicable rules in each and every state in which you are licensed.

Think of Annuities as the Sacrificial Lamb of the Client's Portfolio

Immediate annuities are essentially the sacrificial lamb of the client's portfolio. This colorful description is designed to shift the view of our advisors from an immediate annuity as an inflexible structure to one that handles the burden of filling the retirement income gap, thereby allowing the other assets to live with less investment restrictions. Find ways to present the concept in this way to a few of your clients. I think you will be surprised at how receptive they can be.

[i] Insurance Information Institute. 2017. "Facts + Statistics: Annuities." Individual Immediate Annuity Sales. Insurance Information Institute. https://www.iii.org/fact-statistic/facts-statistics-annuities#Individual%20Immediate%20Annuity%20Sales,%202013-2017%20(1)

[ii] Sandra L. Colby, Jennifer M. Ortman. May 2014. "The Baby Boomer Cohort in the United States: 2012 to 2060." U.S. Department of Commerce, Economics and Statistics Administration, U.S. Census Bureau.

CHAPTER 4

DEFERRED INCOME ANNUITIES – THE NEXT BIG THING

You may have read in the financial press that the deferred income annuity (DIA) is the annuity industry's fastest-growing product type. While this statement is true, technically, it must be taken in context to understand DIAs' actual stature in the marketplace. When showcasing growth rates, it is much easier to post impressive numbers by starting from a small number rather than a large number, and DIAs are definitely starting from a small number. Since 2013, sales of DIAs have gone from about $1 billion per year to close to $3 billion. Despite the impressive 200% growth in six years, this product area still makes up less than 1% of all annuity sales. However, since DIAs can be a valuable retirement planning tool and are increasingly in the news, it's appropriate to dedicate a chapter to this relatively new type of annuity.

What Are They?

A DIA is essentially a deposit (or series of deposits) made onto an annuity contract in the present that will eventually fund a pre-determined amount of income that starts on a specific date in the future. To put it another way, a DIA is an immediate annuity that begins to distribute the income more than 13 months after the contract is purchased. In that sense, it is more of a not-so-immediate annuity. Some professionals refer to them as a personal pension plan because the investor – not a former employer or government entity – funds a future guaranteed income for life with accumulated assets.

How DIA's are Used

DIAs serve two primary functions in retirement strategies. The first is to provide income either at the time of retirement or shortly thereafter, and the second is to layer longevity insurance into a retirement strategy. In terms of the first function, a common goal is to generate a supplemental income stream so that the policyholder can delay receiving Social Security benefits until age 67 or 70. Clients who are pursuing this route are usually in their 50's and want to begin collecting income 6-10 years from the date they purchased the DIA. In fact, according to a MetLife (now Brighthouse Financial) white paper authored by Moshe Milevsky, Ph.D. professor at York University in Toronto, the average age of an individual getting a quote on Cannex's annuity quote engine is 59.25 years. In addition, the average age of the quoted deferral period is just 7.2 years. It's also worth mentioning that the average size of the quoted lump sums is $222,000.[1,2]

The second primary reason for purchasing a DIA is to layer longevity insurance into a retirement plan. The greatest weakness of a retirement plan without a guaranteed income component is that it utilizes systematic withdrawals as a means of stretching accumulated assets for the full duration of retirement. By adding a DIA to the plan, you can predict, with almost 100% certainty, that the client will always receive a check in the mailbox each month. Only the demise of the insurance company providing the annuity and the nullification by the state regulators of some or all of the terms of the contract, events that are highly unlikely, can undermine the income guarantees. When used as longevity insurance, the DIA is typically purchased at or near retirement and the income typically begins at age 80 or 85. Just think about how reassuring it is to structure a retirement portfolio for a client when you know that a "pension" will kick in late in that client's life! Most experts will recommend a systematic withdrawal rate of no more than 4% of a portfolio's principal in order to protect against the risk associated with the sequence of returns. Investors who retired in either 1999 or 2007 learned a hard lesson: Withdrawals have to be modest in order to assure that the portfolio isn't depleted too fast as a result of poor investment performance in the early years of retirement. However, if retirees know that a new stream of income will begin mid-way through retirement, they can withdraw significantly more than 4% initially. It is also possible to take a bit more risk when structuring the portfolio. The inclusion of a DIA to provide longevity insurance might open new opportunities for portfolio construction, so that rather than structuring a portfolio of 50%/50% fixed income and equities, a portfolio could be comprised of 65% equities, 20% fixed income, 15% DIA, as an example.

In the previous chapter, I talked about the objective of utilizing the least amount of capital to fill the retirement income gap. The DIA takes that concept one step further. Because the guaranteed income doesn't start for many years after the purchase date, typically, and often does not need to be paid for as many years (depending upon the income start date), people are often surprised at how little it takes to generate fairly significant sums of money. As an example, based on today's rates of return a 65-year-old male with $184,000 in principal could generate $50,000 of annual income for life beginning at age 80.

Buying Multiple DIAs

One common strategy is to buy multiple DIAs, each with a different start date. Perhaps one kicks in at age 75, another at age 80 and a final one at age 85. The first DIA would provide the bulk of the income and would therefore require the majority of the purchase amount. Since each subsequent DIA would only need to provide enough additional income to maintain the policyholder's standard of living and would start at a later age, it would need a relatively small amount to fund. For example, a 60-year-old client might put $100,000 into a DIA that begins paying **$17,085** per year at age 75. In addition, that same client might put just $15,000 into a DIA that would begin providing an annual income at age 80. The additional $3,785 in income would serve to protect the original income stream from inflation.

Qualified Longevity Annuity Contracts (QLAC's)

In July of 2014, the U.S. Treasury Department issued new rules that introduced the Qualified Longevity Annuity Contract (QLAC) to the public. This rule effectively changed the way DIAs could be treated in qualified plans rather than create a new type of DIA. However, since the Treasury department gave them a new treatment in qualified plans, the industry decided that this was good enough to treat them as a new product type.

It's easy to see how a DIA could be attractive as part of an IRA or 401K. Consider this scenario: The owner of the retirement plan could periodically transfer money into a DIA or multiple DIAs in order to purchase a known future stream of income. The DIA could serve as an alternative investment component along with the customary stocks, bonds or mutual funds.

However, DIAs presented a reporting problem. Required Minimum Distributions have to be based on the value of all the retirement assets. Presumably, this value would include the current value of the DIA even though it technically has no value until the income starts. One could make the argument that since the very goal of the DIA was to pay income over the individual's lifetime it could be excluded from the RMD calculation. Yet the RMD rules about the exclusion were, at best, unclear. The Treasury's ruling about QLACs changed all of that. The new rules state that assets in an IRA invested in a QLAC can be excluded from the RMD calculation. Therefore, by moving IRA money into a QLAC, the investor can both create a future income for life and reduce the total amount of the required annual withdrawal. There are of course limits and rules.

1. A QLAC is limited to the lessor of
    a. 25% of the total qualified plan savings, or
    b. $130,000 (in 2019) - this amount will be adjusted for inflation in increments of $10,000 per adjustment.
2. As long as individual spouses have their own retirement plans, the limits apply separately to each spouse
3. If premium payments ever exceed the premium limits, the excess amounts must be returned to the individual's retirement account in order for the contract to remain a QLAC.
4. The QLAC must start income by the age of 85
5. The QLAC cannot include a variable or indexed annuity contract.
6. The QLAC cannot provide a means to cash out the contract either through commutation or any form of cash surrender value. However, it can provide a lump sum death benefit to a beneficiary equal to any amount of the premiums that have not been paid out in income.
7. Because Roth IRAs are not taxable, Roth IRAs are excluded from the $130,000 and 25% limits.

Although the Treasury department has now opened the door for using DIAs as part of tax-qualified plans, my enthusiasm for these annuities is limited. Significant obstacles remain that must be overcome before they come into popular use. First and foremost, any insurance company that wants to offer these plans must find a way to effectively administer all of the aforementioned rules. In addition, it is not yet clear which party is responsible for managing the premium limits. Since no insurance company will know the total value of an individual's retirement plan, I presume the responsibility rests with the policyholder. But even if that is the case, the insurance company will have to accommodate the return of any excess premiums and will likely want to find a way to protect itself legally from someone trying to game the system. Finally, the broker-dealers that offer these products will want to record the QLAC in the client's account in some way. That means a value of some type will need to be passed from the insurance company to the broker/dealer. Given that the contract cannot have a cash value, there is likely to be some discussion of how this is recorded in the client's account.

So, while QLACs have the potential of becoming an important part of an individual's qualified plan, and certain exclusion and reporting rules could restrain progress in this area in the near future.

Considerations Before Buying A DIA

1. Financial Stability of the Insurance Company

Since your client is funding an income stream that won't be payable for a long time – perhaps 20-25 years – it is essential that you recommend a DIA from only a financially strong insurance company. While the financial crises raised new questions about what a strong insurance looks like, there are a few key traits that can attest to the annuity provider's financial strength and ability to continue operating as a going concern. The provider should be relatively large; it should maintain a relatively high credit rating from one of the major rating agencies; and it should maintain a risk-based capital ratio greater than 350%. Also, look for a company that has a sizeable life insurance block. Life insurance and DIAs (as well as SPIAs) are a natural hedge. If Americans start living longer because we cure catastrophic illnesses like cancer, the higher than expected payments made to owners of SPIAs and DIAs will be offset by the delay of life insurance claims.

2. What if the policyholder dies before the income starts?

If you intend to implement DIAs purely for longevity insurance in a retirement strategy, then a client's unexpected passing will not have a material impact on the dispersal of benefits. In this sense, it is no different than never having a claim on your auto or homeowner's insurance. No one ever refuses to insure their car for fear that they will never have a claim and therefore not get a return on the premiums they paid over the years. In fact, when it comes to property and casualty insurance, everyone hopes they never need the insurance. Yet, when one is "investing" in a DIA, this is often an objection, mostly because they look at it as investment rather than insurance. No one ever wants to lose money on an investment. For this reason, most DIAs come with an option that will pay the beneficiary any unreturned premiums. And in fact, according to MetLife's white paper, 83% of the requested quotes were for an option that provided some kind of payment guarantee tied to the lifetime guarantee. However, such an option will reduce the guaranteed income by about 10%-25%, depending upon the guarantee and the age of the purchaser. After all, one of the reasons a DIA can pay out so much relative to the total premiums paid is the pooling of covered lives, thereby allowing the insurance company to shift excess income from policyholders who die early to increase benefits to those that live longer.

3. Moving the income start date

Some DIAs allow the policyholder to move up the income start date. Of course, the amount of the monthly payout could potentially be adjusted down. Even the most thoughtfully crafted retirement plans can be upset by an unexpected job loss or illness, which is why I recommend this feature.

4. A DIA will likely reduce the policyholder's "assets"

The industry has now agreed on a common format to provide a "value" for both DIAs and immediate annuities, but that does not mean every insurance company and every broker-dealer has the ability to value these types of policies on the client's brokerage statement. In fact, there are many that believe they should not be valued, because it might encourage unwise decision-making. A future income flow certainly has a value in today's dollars, providing that the hypothetical value might encourage the client to monetize it. Of course, it is possible that clients will not add a lot of weight to that factor. Clients don't seem to mind that they don't get a "value" of their Social Security payments or their pension payments. Why should a DIA be any different?

Industry Sales of DIAs Should Be Many Times Current Sales Levels

Despite my lack of enthusiasm about future sales levels of this product, I believe that many clients would benefit greatly by allocating a portion of their fixed income portfolio into a DIA. This is especially true if an individual has a history of longevity within his or her family tree. Consider the following:

1. **Give your clients another "pension"** - One of the greatest fears of the majority of retirees is outliving his or her income. No one wants to have to worry about paying for basic necessities and perhaps becoming a financial burden on their children in order to make ends meet. Studies show that people with a pension lead a far less stressful retirement than those that do not. Give your clients the peace of mind of knowing that yet another quasi-pension check will be coming their way in the future.

2. **Protect your clients from an increase in interest rates** – Common wisdom says that the older one gets; the greater percentage of a client's portfolio should be held in fixed income securities. Of course, this wisdom wasn't fashioned in a world of 2% 10-year Treasury rates. The DIA can serve as a fixed income surrogate. Like a bond, it generates needed cash flow. However, because of the inclusion of mortality credits (benefiting from those that die early), it will provide more cash flow per dollar invested – and if it's a non-qualified asset, at least some of the payment will be a tax-free return of principal. In addition, unlike traditional fixed

income investments the "value" won't decline if interest rates do finally increase over a sustained period of time.

3. **Invest the balance more aggressively** – Regardless of whether interest rates are rising or falling, the longevity insurance provided by the DIA gives you the freedom and flexibility to invest your client's remaining assets more aggressively and accumulate more assets to boost future income streams or provide a legacy to heirs.

Where to Go To Learn More

If I have at least piqued your interest and you want to learn more about how DIAs work and how to efficiently use them in a client's retirement portfolio, I highly recommend Moshe Milevsky's White Paper sponsored by MetLife entitled, *"Bonding with Deferred Income Annuities: Exploring Portfolio Sustainability Options in Retirement"*. Professor Milevsky is not only one of the world's foremost experts on retirement planning, but he also has the rare talent of making complex concepts engaging and easy to understand.

[1,2] *"Bonding with Deferred Income Annuities: Exploring Portfolio Sustainability Options in Retirement"*, by Moshe Milevsky, Ph.D., a white paper sponsored by MetLife, 2015.

[i] Insurance Information Institute. 2017. "Facts + Statistics: Annuities." Individual Immediate Annuity Sales. Insurance Information Institute. https://www.iii.org/fact-statistic/facts-statistics-annuities#Individual%20Immediate%20Annuity%20Sales,%202013-2017%20(1)

[ii] Sandra L. Colby, Jennifer M. Ortman. May 2014. "The Baby Boomer Cohort in the United States: 2012 to 2060." U.S. Department of Commerce, Economics and Statistics Administration, U.S. Census Bureau.

CHAPTER 5

VARIABLE ANNUITIES – ARE THEY REALLY THAT COMPLEX?

I am well aware that in placing the chapter on variable annuities towards the middle of this book I am breaking with conventional thinking. Given the importance of variable annuities, one would think that I would have chosen to present it first. Also, one might have expected this to be a long and relatively complex chapter. After all, FINRA routinely adds variable annuities to its roundup of complex financial products. That perception of complexity underpins almost every article that is critical of variable annuities. Yet a variable annuity itself is a rather simple product: It is all of the optional riders that make it complex – especially the living benefit riders. And since I dedicated a separate chapter to living benefits, this section will be relatively short and simple.

What is a Variable Annuity?

A variable annuity is essentially an assembling of mutual funds wrapped within a tax-deferred annuity structure. Now I suspect that any regulator reading this is cringing at that characterization. They fear that such a description over simplifies and therefore mischaracterizes the product. It does oversimplify it, but I don't believe it mischaracterizes it. Insurance companies began to roll out variable annuities in the early 1980's as the industry's answer to the growing popularity of mutual funds. Sun Life of Canada and Anchor National Life – two of the earliest product's adopters – reasoned that they could offer a "family" of mutual funds with the added benefit of tax deferral. In order to differentiate it as an insurance product, they priced in a return of premium guaranteed death benefit. I put the word "family" in quotes, because the first variable annuities had a very small "family" by today's standards. As an example, Anchor National's American Pathway variable annuity (now owned by AIG/American General), had just five funds, all managed by American Funds – a growth fund, a growth and income fund, a government bond fund, a high yield bond fund and a money market account. But whether the variable annuity has just five funds managed by the same manager or over one hundred funds managed by many managers, it is still really just a collection of mutual funds wrapped within an annuity structure.

Variable Annuity Sub-Accounts

Sub-accounts are an essential component of variable annuities. These are called sub-accounts because the insurance companies that issue variable annuities maintain them within their separate accounts. In addition, tax laws require that in order for variable annuities to maintain their tax-advantaged status, they cannot offer publicly traded mutual funds. Therefore, almost every sub-account within a variable annuity is a mutual fund that was established solely for inclusion into a variable annuity. For obvious reasons, many of these variable annuity sub-accounts are modeled after an existing mutual fund. By that I mean, they typically have the same portfolio managers and are given the same investment objectives [in an attempt to replicate the returns of the publicly traded mutual fund]. However, since these sub-accounts are indeed separate funds, differences in fund size and cash flows often create different performance outcomes from the imitated mutual fund. In fact, the performance of the variable annuity may be better, especially in bull markets. Since variable annuities experience lower turnover than mutual fund money, the portfolio manager may be able to maintain a lower cash position in the variable annuity sub-account than he or she could in the publicly traded mutual fund version.

The Importance of the Separate Account Structure

All insurance companies are required to establish a separate account within which it must place all variable annuity assets that are invested in a mutual fund sub-account. I state it that way because many variable annuities offer a fixed account as an investment option. This option is essentially a fixed annuity option within the variable annuity. Because the rate on this option is fixed and guaranteed by the insurance company, variable annuity assets invested in a fixed account are a general liability obligation of the insurance company and are therefore backed by the company's general account. Prior to the Federal Reserve pushing down interest rates to zero, virtually every variable annuity offered a fixed account option. Today, many insurance companies do not want to offer such an option no matter how low the guaranteed rate.

The financial crisis was a good test of variable annuities' separate account structures. Because the assets within a variable annuity are not part of the insurance company's general account, they are not available to any claims against the insurance company should it get into financial trouble. The separate account structure also prevents the insurance company from co-mingling these funds with its other investments. Just think how nervous the AIG variable annuity policyholders would have been during the financial crises had the separate account structure not existed! Instead, advisors that had AIG variable annuities on their books were able to reassure their clients that their variable annuity investments were not at risk of being turned over to the federal government as part of the bailout agreement. While several notable variable annuity companies had enough financial difficulties to induce them to take TARP money from the Federal Government, their variable annuity policyholders had no reason to panic or liquidate their annuities.

The Guaranteed Death Benefit

We now understand that the undergirding of variable annuity structure helps the product withstand financial market volatility, so let's delve into the death benefit portion. Newer variable annuities structures increasingly omit the guaranteed death benefit, but this feature is still the norm in the industry. Essentially, this benefit states that upon the death of the measuring life, the beneficiary will receive the greater of either the account value at the time the insurance company is notified of the death or the total amount invested, adjusted for cash benefit withdrawals. I have used the phrase "measuring life" because the death benefit can be actuated upon **either** the passing of the policy owner **or** the annuitant, depending upon whether or not it is an owner or annuitant driven contract. Make sure you always understand which life will trigger the death benefit before you complete a variable annuity application. Better yet, always recommend that the owner and the annuitant are the same person to avoid unnecessary complications.

Over the years, variable annuity critics have often taken the position that this guaranteed death benefit is really not worth much. The reasoning behind this criticism is that one would expect the value of the underlying sub-accounts to be worth more than the amount invested by the time the policyholder dies. In my view, much like any other type of insurance, the variable annuity death benefit isn't worth much until unexpected and potentially dire circumstances present themselves. For this reason, many experienced financial advisors felt a sense of vindication and poetic justice when Suze Orman came up against this very issue when a caller wondered why a variable annuity death benefit is not a good thing when it paid her so much extra money after her husband unexpectedly died. You can find this video on YouTube at the link below:

http://www.youtube.com/watch?v=rd_3nCENMT8 (Suze Orman's Bad Call)

While no one hopes to need the guaranteed death benefit, it's very reassuring to know that it is there. In fact, the insurance industry paid out hundreds of millions of dollars in death benefit claims after both the tech crash of 2000-2002 and the financial crises of 2007-2009. Certainly, the beneficiaries of those policies were glad to have the feature. And today, after the one of the longest bull market runs in history, older variable annuity policyholders can rest well knowing that money invested into a variable annuity will pay their beneficiary no less than the amount invested should they die shortly after the next bear market begins.

On all policies issued today, the guaranteed death benefit is adjusted pro-rata by any withdrawals. As an example, if the death benefit is $100,000 and the account value is only $80,000, an $8,000, or 10%, withdrawal will reduce the death benefit by 10% as well. Therefore, in this example the $8,000 withdrawal will reduce the death benefit by $10,000. Insurance companies do this in order to ensure that they always reduce the death benefit in proportion to the account value. That was not always the case, however. Many contracts issued prior to 2003 had death benefits that were reduced by the same dollar amount as the withdrawals rather than the same percentage.

If you have a client that has a death benefit that is reduced dollar for dollar, make sure that client holds onto that policy! It can be extremely valuable under the right circumstances. Let's explore that concept through what I believe is a compelling illustration.

Total Premiums: $100,000

Death Benefit: $100,000

Account Value (due to market decline): $75,000

Withdrawal taken from account value: $70,000

Account Value after withdrawal: $5,000

Death Benefit after withdrawal: $30,000

You now have just $5,000 supporting a $30,000 death benefit. In reality, you could withdraw even more of the account value. You just need to make sure the account value is large enough that it will never go to $0 after fees and potential market loses. If it goes to $0, then the death benefit is eliminated. You can see that such a contract, under the right circumstances, can basically give the policyholder free term insurance (the death benefit) while still reinvesting most of the account value in a different investment. In addition, some of these policies have enhanced death benefits that either grow at a certain percentage each year, and/or capture the highest policy anniversary. In such cases, the death benefit can grow even if the account value falls. Therefore, any significant drop in the market can create a situation where it may make financial sense (for the policyholder, not the insurance company), to strip a non-qualified annuity of most of its account value.

I strictly limit this advice to non-qualified annuities because Reg. 1.401(a)(9)-6 of the internal revenue code requires variable annuity companies to include the present value of the death benefit in the calculation of the required minimum distribution of an IRA. Therefore, if a policyholder strips out a variable annuity in an IRA, it is highly likely that the RMD will cause the policy to be liquidated before the policyholder dies, thereby eliminating the death benefit.

Let's go back to the example used above of how the policy with the $100,000 death benefit was reduced dollar for dollar to show how this problem could occur. If the policy has a $5,000 account value and a $30,000 death benefit, the RMD would be calculated on the $5,000 account value plus the present value of the incremental $25,000 in death benefit. If the client is in her late 70's, the RMD could be as much as $3,500, or 70% of the account value. If so, then the policy is going to be liquidated within two years. Once the policy is liquidated, the death benefit goes away.

Enhanced Death Benefits

Many variable annuities come with enhanced death benefit features that can be added to a contract for an additional fee. The cost of these features used to be quite modest, but insurance companies realized how expensive these features could be during the financial crises of 2007-09. A number of companies responded to this by dropping these features from the products. The companies that continued to offer them did so at significantly higher costs. Despite this, these features can be very beneficial to a policyholder that has the goal of maximizing the legacy to the beneficiary rather than generating retirement income. All of these benefits are reduced proportionally by any withdrawals.

Important note: All of these options will increase the death benefit only up to a specified age – usually 80 or 85. Once the measured life (typically the policyholder) reaches that age, the death benefit value is locked into place. The most common enhanced death benefits are as follows:

1. Highest Policy Anniversary Death Benefit

This option pays the beneficiary the greater of the standard return of premium death benefit or the highest policy anniversary value. This has the effect of moving the death benefit up as the contract value increases. Then if the contract value subsequently falls, the beneficiary is still entitled to the higher value. Think about how valuable such a benefit would have been to a beneficiary that received a death benefit in 2009 on a contract that was purchased in 2003.

2. A death benefit that increases by a given percentage per year

This option increases the death benefit by a specified percentage per year – typically about five percent to six percent. This allows you to assure that client that the beneficiary will receive a minimum pre-determined amount provided there are no withdrawals and the contract is not annuitized.

3. Combination of options 1 and 2

Can't decide between the highest policy anniversary death benefit and one that increases by a specified percentage? Consider one that combines the two. With this option, the beneficiary receives the greater of the highest policy anniversary value or the original premium growing at the specified amount. Of course, both values are adjusted pro-rata by any withdrawals. Not surprisingly, this is the most expensive of all of the death benefit options.

How Annuitization Affects Death Benefits

At this point, we should discuss one of the most important aspects of variable annuities: <u>The death benefit goes away of the contract is annuitized.</u> You absolutely must keep this reality foremost in your thoughts when talking to your clients about the value of death benefits on these products. Indeed, this fact applies to any type of annuity, but since account values are most likely to diminish on variable annuities, the death benefits become a critical feature.

<u>You</u> might believe that you do not intend to annuitize the contracts, so the loss of the death benefit is irrelevant to my practice. However, virtually every insurance company today has an age at which they require annuitization. This age can be as low as 85 and as high as 100. If the policyholder reaches that age, the contract will be annuitized and any additional death benefit will be lost. Most policyholders will

choose to avoid annuitizing the contract by liquidating the contract. However, such a choice will obviously also terminate the death benefit.

Variable Annuity Fees

Behind only complexity, the second biggest criticism of variable annuities is typically about the "excessive fees". So, are variable annuities prohibitively expensive, and what do these fees cover? Let's start with an explanation of the typical fees.

Mortality and Expense Charge: This fee is typically 1% -1.7% per year depending upon the share class that is purchased. Most variable annuity literature will describe this as necessary to cover the costs associated with the guaranteed death benefit and support the income (annuitization) guarantees associated with the contract. The prospectus typically describes the cost in this manner, leading critics to hold the opinion that the fees are to cover these benefits are excessive. However, the reality is that only a portion of this total expense covers these guarantees – perhaps 0.15% to 0.30%. The rest covers the cost of issuing the contract and provides the insurance company's profit. What are the costs of issuing the contract? Mostly it's the commission that is paid to the selling agent and the costs of wholesaling the annuity. However, it also covers the cost to actually issue the contract and pay for any additional marketing expenses, such as literature and product promotions.

Annual Administrative Costs – In addition to the annual Mortality and Expense charge, there is often an annual administrative cost of about 0.15%. This covers the cost of servicing the contract each year, including mailing quarterly statements and annual prospectuses.

Sub-Account Fees – Since the sub-accounts are merely funds established for use in a variable annuity, the related fees compensate the portfolio manager. Typically, the insurance company serves as the advisor to the fund and the fund company serves as the sub-advisor. This allows the insurance company to share in the fees charged for each of the sub-accounts. This is a very important source of revenue to the insurance company. The mortality and expense and admin fees are typically set to mostly cover all of the assumed initial and ongoing costs of the product. Therefore, the insurance company's portion of the sub-account fees generates much of the profits of the product.

For any variable annuities sold on a commission basis, the total cost of the variable annuity will always be greater than the mutual fund it is patterned after. This is due to the simple reason that a mutual fund only needs to pay two parties – the fund company and the distributor. The variable annuity needs to pay three parties – the fund company, the distributor and the insurance company. What you as the seller of a variable annuity need to decide is whether or not the additional costs are worth the two primary benefits not found in a mutual fund – tax deferral and the death benefit guarantee. The insurance companies will likely claim that I am ignoring the benefits of providing an income you can't outlive via the annuitization of the contract. While I'm a big believer in the benefits of variable annuitization, the reality is that virtually no one annuitizes these contracts. Therefore, I don't believe that touting a seldom-used feature is a strong argument – even if it is a feature that advisors should invoke more often.

Variable Annuity Share Classes

Variable annuities might not consistently invoke the annuitization feature, but they all offer policyholders a choice from a range of share classes. The early variable annuities were all B-share contracts that typically carried a five-year contingent deferred sales charge, usually referred to as a surrender charge. I would love to find out whose brilliant idea it was to label this charge a "surrender charge". Clearly, that person never considered the fact that no one likes to "surrender" and everyone hates a "charge". Since the industry continues to embrace the term despite the misleading connotation, in order to avoid confusion, I will refer to this charge as a "surrender charge" throughout the book.

1. B-shares

A B-share variable annuity will not have a front-end sales charge and will typically have a surrender charge that amortizes over five to seven years. Each premium payment will carry its own surrender charge period. Since the charge is designed to recover the acquisition costs of the contract (commission, wholesaler comp, marketing costs and policy issue costs), it will typically start at about 1% more than the highest possible initial compensation and then drop by 1% per year. For example, if the contract has a commission option that pays 7% without a trail, the surrender charge will likely start at 8%. The annual mortality and expense, or M&E, cost associated with a B-share will typically range from 1%-1.35%. B-shares make up about 2/3 of all variable annuity sales.

2. L-shares

Like a B-share, an L-share has no upfront sales charge, but typically has a surrender charge. The difference is that the latter has a surrender charge of only three to four years. Because the surrender charge is shorter than that of a B-share, the annual M&E is typically 0.3%-0.4% higher than a B-share. The insurance company needs this extra revenue to compensate for the fact that L-shares tend to be liquidated sooner than B-shares, thereby giving the insurance company fewer years to recover its upfront acquisition costs.

L-shares were a very popular option when insurance companies were continually introducing new and improved living benefits – a practice that came to a grinding halt in 2009. The strategy back then was to buy a short surrender product and then exchange that contract for one that had the latest and greatest living benefit when the surrender charge ended. By 2005, L-shares were about 50% of all variable annuity sales. Many broker-dealers saw L-shares capture almost 70% of their sales. However, in an environment where new living benefit structures

provide diminishing benefits, it's difficult to see how anyone could justify an L-share being
purchased if a living benefit is added to the contract. In order to benefit from a living benefit, the policyholder must own the contract for his or her entire life. If the contract is ever surrendered, the policyholder has essentially paid for an option that was never used. Since the higher fees continue beyond the surrender charge period, how can one justify requiring the policyholder to pay up to 0.4% more in annual fees to simply shorten the surrender charge by a few years? As regulators have increasingly asked this question over the last couple of year, the market share captured by this share class has declined significantly. In fact, today this share class is practically extinct.

3. C-shares

C-shares have no upfront sales charge and no surrender charge. Since C-shares can be cashed in at any time with no charge, obviously this share class will carry a much lower commission. They typically pay a 1% to 2% upfront commission and an annual trail of up to 1%. The liquidity offered by a C-share comes at a cost. The annual M&E typically runs 1.7%-1.85%, but an increasing number of C-shares are being introduced with lower commissions and an M&E expense of 1.3%-1.4%. This share class makes sense for clients who choose not to add a living benefit and value liquidity.

4. A-shares

A-shares charge an upfront sales charge based on the size of the total investment. Since the fees are deducted upfront, A-shares do not have a surrender charge. A handful of variable annuity companies created this share class design at the request of Edward Jones. Jones believed that since insurance companies designed variable annuities to be long-term holdings the policyholder would end up paying less in total fees with an A-share design. While this is indeed the case, the popularity of living benefits caused Jones to mostly abandon this share class as an option. Because the income benefit base of the living benefit is based on the invested premium, the upfront sales charge caused the policyholder to start the guarantee income on an income base that was less than the amount of the purchase.

5. O-shares

In 2011, Edward Jones replaced the A-shares they were offering with O-shares. This share class breaks the annual contract charges into two pieces:

1) An annual insurance contract charge of typically 0.85%

2) A premium-based charge that is assessed for a seven-year period after the premium is deposited into the contract. This charge has breakpoints at different premium levels, but typically ranges from 0.70% at $50,000 or less and 0.15% for $1 million or more.

The idea behind the O-share is to reduce the annual fee to the client once the insurance company has recouped its cost to issue the contract. Most clients will pay a little more for the first seven years, but will then pay much less after the premium-based charge drops off.

6. Bonus Annuities

A bonus annuity is really a B-share annuity where the insurance company adds money to the initial premium – typically 3% to 6% of the initial purchase - when the policy is issued. As an example, if a policyholder invests $100,000 into a 5% bonus annuity, the insurance company will issue a contract for $105,000. Insurance companies are not in the business of giving away money, therefore the bonus comes at a cost. The insurance company recovers the cost of the bonus over time by a) paying slightly lower broker commissions, b) charging a higher M&E, and c) issuing the contract with a higher surrender charge and a longer surrender charge period (typically nine years). It's better to think of a bonus as a loan from the insurance company to the policyholder. The policyholder gets to invest the loaned amount (the bonus) into the selected sub-accounts and keep the earnings from the loan. The policyholder pays the loan back over time in the form of higher contract fees.

American Skandia introduced the bonus annuity as a way to induce investors to do 1035 exchanges. Of course, Skandia's marketing literature never described it that way, but for all practical purposes, that was the intent of the share class. The bonus became a means to justify exchanging a contract that would still incur a surrender charge. As long as the bonus was greater than the remaining surrender charge on the existing annuity, the policyholder could be told that he or she would benefit financially from cashing in the existing contract for a new one even after the surrender charge was deducted. Not surprisingly, the regulators eventually took a dim view of this practice. They immediately became suspect of any 1035 exchange into a bonus contract and eventually began to have a negative view of any bonus variable annuity sale. The sad part of all of this is that when used appropriately, a bonus annuity is often the best choice for the policyholder. In many contracts, the bonus is sufficiently healthy to offset more than a dozen years of higher fees – even after the higher surrender charges. Therefore, unless the policyholder is confident that he or she will own the contract for at least 15 years, in many cases the bonus annuity will generate the highest account value of all of the share classes. Now don't get me wrong: I am *not advocating* for using bonus annuities as a means to do 1035 exchanges. In fact, where a bonus annuity is likely to be the best choice is for the first contract a client ever buys. Why not choose the contract that will provide the highest account value even after surrender charges for the first 12- to 15-years of the contract?

7. Advisory annuities

Variable annuity companies have tried for years to successfully market no-load annuities to be used in fee-based accounts. These annuities pay no commission and therefore have no surrender charge. Since the insurance company does not have to recover any commission costs, the M&E typically runs only 0.20% to 0.60%. If the product is sold directly to consumers by an insurance company that markets directly to consumers, then the cost will be even lower since the company has the economy of scale to offset any wholesaling costs. Its marketing costs are also lower. One of the initial designs was an annuity that had no M&E costs at all. The only charge was a monthly fee of $20. This product is sold mostly by RIAs. How can an insurance company make money by charging only $20 per month? It goes back to my earlier comments about the advisor and sub-advisor relationship. The $20 per month covers its ongoing administrative costs. The profits come from their share of the sub-account fee.

Although several insurance companies and a few broker-dealers have tried to promote the idea of selling variable annuities in fee-based accounts, total sales continue to be an insignificant percentage of total industry sales. This has surprised me a bit. One of the biggest challenges to selling variable annuities is the compliance requirements at each broker-dealer. How can a regulator object to a product selection that pays no commission, has extremely low fees and is totally liquid for the duration of the contract? Logic would dictate that advisory annuities should be readily accepted by the regulators and therefore should pretty much fly through any compliance approval process. After all, if the advisor is not receiving a commission for the sale, he or she has no incentive to recommend an annuity over any other investment. It becomes even less problematic if there is no surrender charge to get out of the annuity. Unfortunately, thus far, the regulators have been reluctant to carve out this share class for special suitability treatment.

In addition, the recent attempt to move all financial advisors to the Department of Labor's fiduciary standard prompted many advisors to adopt an exclusively a fee-based business model. Although a federal court allowed the Rule to be vacated, the prospect of the Rule added to the industry's motivation to fully integrate this share class into their businesses. In fact, since 2017, we have seen a record number of fee-based annuities come to market.

So why don't no-load variable annuities capture a larger share of the market? I think there are several reasons. To begin with, there are much fewer contract choices. Up until recently, the insurance companies and the broker-dealers rarely promoted them. Many advisors simply do not know how to position these products into an advisory portfolio. Second, they often do not work particularly well with the mechanics of the fee-based account. Most broker-dealers will have trouble including the product in any performance analysis of the account. And then there is the issue of the annual asset fee. For tax reasons and the need to preserve the full value of any living benefit, you don't ever want to take the fee from the annuity itself. The biggest reason that advisors don't sell no-load variable annuities, perhaps, is because the math suggests that most no-load annuities do not save the client much money, it at all. If you add a 1% fee to a no-load annuity costing 0.5% per year, you have a fee that is very close to a c share variable annuity.

No-load annuities provide valuable insights into the true cost structure of variable annuities. If an insurance company offers a no-load annuity at a cost of 0.5% and offers a B-share contract with identical features at a cost of 1.3%, then you know that the commissions are priced into the B-share contract at a cost of 0.8% per year.

Investment Only Variable Annuities

Jackson National's Elite Access was the first of what soon became many investment only variable annuities. There is no agreed upon definition of an investment only variable annuity. However, it is generally understood to be a variable annuity that does not offer a living benefit option and may or may not offer a guaranteed death benefit. Therefore, the contract is sold primarily for the ability to buy a collection of sub-accounts on a tax-deferred basis. I find this new trend to be more than a bit strange because under the definition that I have posited here, every variable annuity sold prior to the introduction of living benefits would have been an investment only variable annuity. For that matter, contracts that offer living benefits could qualify as investment-only if the policyholder elects not to add a living benefit to the contract. It seems like insurance companies are merely repackaging an existing concept. To be fair, these contracts typically have three or four unique characteristics. But then, if the goal is to repackage an existing concept, then by definition the policy must offer providers a product with distinct differences. I've listed the differences below. Decide for yourself just how unique these new investment-only variable annuities really are.

1. The inclusion of alternative mutual funds_– While variable annuities have traditionally offered policyholders a wide variety of funds, this range of choices has mostly boiled down to different managers, each offering his or her own version of stock and bond funds. Jackson National elected to differentiate its investment only variable annuity to a great extent by highlighting less traditional asset classes such as alternative mutual funds.

2. Lower fees, lower commissions and shorter surrender charges – The M&E charge on most investment-only variable annuities is 15-30 basis points less than a traditional B-share variable annuity. In addition, most insurance companies are attempting to differentiate the product by shortening the surrender charge by a couple of years. Needless to say, if both the M&E is less and the surrender charge is shorter, the insurance company cannot afford to pay as much commission. Therefore, the commission tends to be 1% to 1.5% less than the traditional B-share and often carries a lower trail as well.

3. Guaranteed Death Benefit is Optional (if offered at all) – Most of these annuities offer a return of premium death benefit as an option for an additional cost. Many don't offer this feature at all.

4. A Simpler Product – When you eliminate living benefits, and possible death benefits, as an option, you most definitely simplify the product. The client brochure and the prospectus both become less confusing and therefore much shorter. In addition, you reduce disclosure requirements significantly.

Variable Annuity or Mutual Fund?

Ever since variable annuities were first introduced to the market, professionals have debated the merits of a variable annuity versus that of a mutual fund. For much of the past 10 years, this debate was mostly pushed to the sidelines by the living benefits that were usually added to a variable annuity contract. Now that an increasing number of insurance companies are introducing investment-only variable annuities, however, this debate has returned to the forefront. Neither product has a clear and decisive advantage over the other; therefore, the appropriate choice depends upon the financial and emotional needs of the client. With that in mind, let's look at the most common arguments against a variable annuity as the product of choice.

1. Mutual Funds are Cheaper

As noted earlier, an extra party is involved in the variable annuity (the insurance company) structure; therefore, it will always be more expensive than investing solely into mutual funds. The questions that remains are whether the tax deferral and guaranteed death benefit (assuming there is one) are worth the additional cost? Also, don't underestimate the behavioral finance benefits that can come with the variable annuity. The structure of the variable annuity leads policyholders to more likely stick with the original investment plan. In short, variable annuity assets are better able to retain funds than mutual funds. This is particularly true if there is a living benefit or death benefit on the contract, or both.

2. Mutual funds are taxed more favorably

For non-qualified assets, mutual funds do indeed create the opportunity for long-term capital gains. In addition, they provide a stepped-up cost basis at death. Variable annuities are always taxed as ordinary income when the funds are distributed, even at death. However, mutual funds can create some unpleasant tax situations that variable annuities avoid. First of all, mutual funds throw off taxable income each year even if the shareholder did not take any liquidate any shares. In addition, a good portion of these gains is likely to be short-term capital gains. And who enjoys explaining to a client why they have a taxable gain on a mutual fund position that has actually declined in value – something that can happen if the market falls shortly after the fund is purchased? Finally, the statistics indicate that the average holding period for a mutual fund is about 18 months. Therefore, many shareholders are creating short-term capital gains by reallocating their mutual fund assets. Variable annuity policyholders can transfer funds from one sub-account to another without generating a taxable event. This can be a particularly attractive feature after a lengthy bull run like we are experiencing today. As equity values climb, clients can quickly become over weighted in stocks. Rebalancing the portfolio typically leads to realizing capital gains. However, if the client owns a variable annuity, funds can be moved into more conservative sub-accounts without creating a taxable event.

In addition, the taxable earnings from a mutual fund are subject to the 3.8% investment income tax that was introduced to help pay for the

Patient Protection and Affordable Care Act, popularly known as ObamaCare. As long as the earnings from the annuity remain deferred, it is not included in this calculation. For clients that are close to the $250,000 income threshold for this tax, the annuity can be a good alternative.

But what about the stepped-up cost basis at death? The annual distributions from the fund companies cause the cost basis to continually adjust upward. Therefore, this attractive tax break is likely to be muted over time for a mutual fund investment.

Simply put, there is something very reassuring in knowing that you are not going to get a 1099 on a particular investment until you actually decide to make a withdrawal. It certainly simplifies the tax reporting.

3. Variable annuities make no sense in qualified plans

As I stated earlier in this chapter, once you put a variable annuity into a qualified plan, it obviously loses the advantages of tax deferral. Given that, why would anyone ever put a variable annuity into a qualified plan rather than a mutual fund? Two reasons stand out. First and foremost are the living and death benefit guarantees that are not offered by mutual funds. Sometimes just the addition of a return of premium death benefit (or an enhanced death benefit) is enough to get a client comfortable with allocating more of his or her retirement money into equities. But it's the living benefit that can really make the difference. When you strip it down, a living benefit is nothing more than a systematic withdrawal that is guaranteed for life by the insurance company. An individual retirement account is the one asset from which every client must take withdrawals from even if they don't want to. So why not add a benefit that guarantees those withdrawals will continue even if they cause the policy to liquidate?

Absent a living or death benefit guarantee, the only reason I can see for justifying a variable annuity in a qualified account rather than a mutual fund is a unique mix of investment options. Many variable annuities offer sub-account options that cannot be purchased on a retail basis. Others offer strategies to automatically allocate the policyholder's money amongst the various sub-accounts. However, these often come with a relatively high cost, so always be mindful of what the policyholder must pay for these options.

4. Mutual funds are simpler

It's hard to argue with this one. Variable annuities are classified as complex products and mutual funds are not for good reason. And of course, once the regulators classify a product as "complex," with it will comes greater compliance oversight. Finally, variable annuities come with applications that, due to regulatory disclosure requirements, can run up to 20 pages long or longer.

My conclusion

The choice between a mutual fund and a variable annuity can be a wrenching one. I prefer to find uses for both investment vehicles in clients' portfolios. While many clients own mutual funds but no variable annuities, few clients own variable annuities in place of mutual funds. Adding both to a portfolio makes perfect sense to me. While I view both as long-term investments within my portfolio, I take a very personal approach to prioritizing how to use them. For the most part, I plan to tap into my mutual fund money long before I access my variable annuity money. The exception will be years where I have relatively low taxable income. Those will be the best years to recognize the tax deferred income from the annuity. The bottom line is that by having both taxable and tax deferred assets, I can coordinate withdrawals to minimize my taxes. In addition, when it is time to move from the accumulation phase to the withdrawal phase, the variable annuity money will provide the backbone of my retirement income. After all, that is what an annuity is really designed to do. My mutual fund money will be used to supplement that income as needed.

Oh, and one last thing about the variable annuity I own: It sure is nice not to get a 1099 every tax year!

CHAPTER 6

STRUCTURED ANNUITIES – WHAT ARE THEY AND WHERE DO THEY FIT?

Not long after the Financial Crisis of 2007-2008, AXA introduced Structured Capital Strategies, the industry's first structured annuity. A few years later, Brighthouse Financial (at the time, MetLife) and Allianz followed with their own offerings. Strong sales growth is now bringing other carriers into the marketplace. These contracts are typically filed as variable annuities and the returns are always tied to an index. They are sometimes referred to as indexed variable annuities. However, since they are essentially structured notes with an annuity wrapper, I will refer to them as structured annuities.

What Are They?

Versatility is the hallmark of structured annuities. Insurance companies can offer a wide variety of the products, so I could probably write several chapters on all of the various options and how they work. Ultimately, structured annuities all adhere to one constant: They require the policyholder to make three choices that are essentially the same as an indexed annuity:

1. The duration of the interest crediting segment – typically from one to six years
2. The index used to determine account value performance (i.e., the S&P 500 or the MSCI EAFE)
3. The crediting method – a cap on earnings, a participation rate or a spread deducted to calculate the final return.

Unlike an indexed annuity, however, the policyholder also has to choose the amount and type of downside protection. The potential upside decreases relative to the amount of downside protection the policyholder elects to put on the policy.

The benchmark index, in addition to the chosen time period, subject to a cap or percentage on the upside, determines the actual return. If you are thinking that this sounds like an index annuity, then you are correct – except for one very important difference. In a structured annuity, the policyholder could receive less than his or her invested principal. How much less is determined by the policyholder based on his or her risk tolerance. In exchange for the additional risk of loss, the policyholder has significantly more upside potential. Typically, structured annuities will offer two methods of limiting downside exposure:

1. "Buffer" against loss

Structured annuities typically come with several "buffer" choices of 10 percent, 20 percent, or 30 percent. This percentage represents the total amount of downside protection. For example, if the policyholder selects a 10 percent buffer, then the policyholder is protected against any loss as long as the chosen index does not decline more than 10 percent. Therefore, if the index over the selected period created a return of -15 percent, the policyholder would only incur a loss of five percent. Similarly, if the policyholder selects a buffer of 20 percent, then no loss occurs unless the index would result in a loss of more than 20 percent. Not surprisingly, the larger the buffer, the lower the upside potential. Actual pricing may look as follows:

Example #1:
Time Period: three years
Index: S&P 500
Buffer: 10 percent
Cap on performance of the index over the three-year period: 24 percent.

As a further example, let's assume a client invests $100,000 when the S&P 500 is at 2,500. If three years later the index is at 2,000 (down 20%), then the client's investment will be lower by 10%, or $90,000 (since the insurance company absorbs the first 10% of the loss). If, however, the index value climbs to 3,250, an increase of 30%, the client's $100,000 would be worth $124,000 due to the 24% cap.

Example #2:

Time Period: six years

Index: S&P 500

Buffer: 10 percent

Cap on performance of the index over the six-year period: 80 percent (due to the longer time period, relative to example #1)

Buffer: 25 percent (same period and index)

Cap on performance of the index over the six-year period: 40 percent (due to the higher buffer than above)

You can clearly see from these rate examples, how the upside potential is enhanced by either increasing the term and/or reducing the downside protection. Obviously, the opposite is true as well. The more the protection desired by the client and/or the shorter the term selected, the lower the potential upside.

2. "Guard Strategy"

This method uses tactics that are opposite to the "buffer" method. With a "guard strategy" option, the policyholder is exposed to the percentage loss up to the guarded amount, but is protected against any loss after the guard percentage. For example, if the policyholder selects a 10 percent guard, then he or she is subject to a loss of up to 10 percent. If the index over the selected period of time creates a loss of more than 10 percent, then the insurance company covers the loss beyond the 10 percent. The appeal of this strategy is that the policyholder knows the maximum possible loss during the period selected. The potential upside decreases in relation to increases of guards that the policyholder selects. Actual pricing may look as follows:

Example:

Period: one-year

Index: S&P 500

Guard: 10 percent

Cap on performance of the index over the 1-year period: 10.75 percent

The biggest difference between the buffer strategy and the guard strategy is the potential downside risk. A client that wants to lock in a known maximum loss would likely be more interested in the guard strategy, while a client that wants only wants to reduce the loss in exchange for a higher potential return would likely lean towards the buffer strategy.

So now we have covered the two methods of limiting downside exposure on a structured annuity. Of course, there is more to structured annuities than managing investment risk.

How Fees and Spreads Affect Overall Returns

Like indexed annuities, some structured annuities offer options that have higher participation rates in exchange for an annual fee or spread. This additional cost is deducted from any gains. The idea behind this approach is to provide more upside in the years where the index performs well above historic averages. Policyholders essentially pay for this privilege by accepting lower returns in years when the index is positive but below historic averages. Back testing would indicate that over the long run, the fee/spread options should provide a boost on the overall average return. However, it will also lead to a wider expected range of possible returns.

Who Should Consider a Structured Annuity?

While a couple of structured annuities have now come to market with a living benefit, this product type is still bought almost solely as a means to participate in the market upside with some protection on the downside. In fact, they are typically priced under the assumption that the policyholder only holds the policy through the surrender charge period. Therefore, while, like all other types of annuities, policyholders have the option to annuitize structured annuities, they are not typically purchased as a source of retirement income. They are only about tax-deferred growth. This makes structured annuities an appropriate option for an individual that says they want to be in the market, but you know they will be calling you the first time the market drops more than 5%. I call these clients "chicken equity" buyers.

CHAPTER 7

HOW NON-QUALIFIED ANNUITIES ARE TAXED

In order to protect myself, I'm going to preface this chapter with the statement that I am not a tax attorney and therefore the information in this chapter should not be considered tax advice. This is merely my understanding of how annuities are taxed based on my thirty-five years in the annuity industry. Please consult a tax expert before making any decisions that could impact the tax situation of any of your clients. Now, having gotten that disclaimer out of the way, let's address the topic at hand.

Annuities held in a qualified plan are always taxed according to the rules of that particular qualified plan. There is nothing unique to the taxation simply because the qualified plan asset is held in an annuity. Therefore, this chapter will focus solely on how annuities are taxed in non-qualified plans.

Taxation Due to a Withdrawal From the Contract

All annuities are taxed as ordinary income as income is distributed from the contract. There is no capital gains or stepped up cost basis at death. This is the trade-off Congress set in exchange for tax deferred treatment. In addition, annuities are taxed on a Last-In-First-Out (LIFO) basis. Therefore, to the extent there are earnings in the contract, the earnings come out first. There is one exception to this rule, although those exceptions are exceedingly rare. Prior to the Tax Equity and Fiscal Responsibility Act (TEFRA) of 1982 (has there ever been a more inaccurate name for a tax act?), annuities were taxed on a First-In-First-Out basis (FIFO). Congress grandfathered all existing contracts. Therefore, contracts issued prior to August 14, 1982, are still taxed on a FIFO basis. In addition, that tax treatment carried over into any new annuities purchased by the FIFO contract as the result of a 1035 exchange. If you happen to stumble across a FIFO annuity contract, treat it like gold. The lucky owners of these contracts can take out their entire original premium payments before they have to worry about taxes or penalties.

It's important to understand that all taxable income is the responsibility of the owner even if the income is paid to someone other than the owner. This happens most often when a contract is annuitized and the annuitant is different than the owner, but it can also happen when the owner instructs the insurance company to make withdrawals payable to someone else. The owner cannot escape this rule even if the payments are payable to a charity – although he would be eligible for a tax deduction for the contributions.

An Annuity Can Create A Taxable Loss

If a policyholder buys an annuity and receives less than he or she invested, the policyholder is entitled to report the "loss" as a deduction against ordinary income. The tax code is not clear as to where a taxpayer should claim the loss on Form 1040. The most conservative approach is to treat it as a miscellaneous itemized deduction not subject to the 2% of AGI floor. A more aggressive approach is to take the loss under the "other gains or losses" on the front of the 1040. Given the uncertainty, the policy owner should obviously consult his or her tax advisor. Typically, a loss on annuity is only likely to occur on a variable annuity. This, of course, would occur if the value of the chosen sub-accounts decline in value and the contract is liquidated. This could also occur with a structured annuity, but the downside protection provided by the contract structure should keep this from being a frequent occurrence. With a fixed or indexed annuity, the only way a loss should ever be incurred is if the policyholder cashes in the policy shortly after it's purchased thereby triggering a surrender charge and/or market value adjustment to be greater than the credited interest at the time of the withdrawal.

The Aggregation Rule

After TEFRA became law, some clever insurance companies attempted to get around the law by offering to issue multiple contracts. One company went as far as offering to break the premium into individual contracts as small as $1,000. All you had to do was check a box on the application and the insurance company took care of the rest. How did this concept work? Let's look at an example.

Let's say a client named Jim Smith has $100,000 to invest. If Mr. Smith put the principal in one annuity and then earns $50,000 in deferred income, he would have a contract that has a basis of $100,000 and $50,000 of reportable income. Since the contract is LIFO, Mr. Smith would be responsible for paying taxes on the first $50,000 withdrawn. But what if Mr. Smith bought ten individual $10,000 contracts instead? Assuming he still earned $50,000 in reportable income, he would have ten contracts each with $10,000 in basis and $5,000 in income. If Mr. Smith needed $45,000, I could cash in three $15,000 contracts and receive $30,000 in principal and $15,000 in reportable income. If Mr. Smith had only one contract, all $45,000 would be taxable to him. On the other hand, if Mr. Smith wanted to report as much income as possible – perhaps because he was in a low tax bracket that year - he could simply make a partial withdrawal of income from all 10 contracts.

Once Congress caught on to this game, they passed the aggregation rule as part of the 1988 tax change. The aggregation rule states that multiple non-qualified annuity contracts issued to the same owner by the same company in the same calendar year are treated as though they are one contract for tax purposes. Therefore, if Mr. Smith buys an annuity from XYZ Insurance Company on February 1 and then buys another from the same company on December 1 of the same year, XYZ will report all withdrawals as though these 2 contracts are really one contract. However, if Mr. Smith waits until January of the following year to purchase the second contract, then they are deemed to be two contracts for tax purposes. The same year and same company requirements of this rule were put in place solely for ease of administration. Clearly, it would be impossible for two different insurance companies to coordinate tax reporting; therefore, this rule is avoided if the policyholder buys one contract from XYZ Insurance Company and then a second one from ABC Insurance Company. In addition, it's difficult for any insurance company to link multiple contracts within their own company for tax reporting purposes only. It's easier if they only have to worry about one calendar year, therefore this was the compromise that was reached when the law was crafted.

This of course means there is still a way to more efficiently manage the taxes on annuity withdrawals. The example I used above is still possible even under today's aggregation rule. It just means your client has to buy contracts from multiple companies rather than a single contract with a single company.

Taxes At Death

TEFRA also specified death at distribution rules upon the "death of the holder" of the annuity. Unfortunately, the tax code does not define who the "holder" is – although it is presumed to be the owner. The tax code also seems to presume that the owner and the annuitant are always the same, because there is no language as to what must happen if the annuitant and the owner are two different people and the annuitant dies prior to the owner. This ambiguity has caused more than a few tax problems for poorly structured annuity contracts and death benefit decisions that are made without understanding the requirements of this rule. But before I get into that, let's take a look at what must happen upon the "death of the holder".

The tax code states that when the "holder" dies, a spousal beneficiary has 4 options and a non-spousal beneficiary has 3 options.

Spousal Beneficiary Options:

1. Continue the contract as the new owner of the contract. This is the same concept of the spouse taking the ownership of a deceased spouse's IRA. The spouse would simply become the new owner and would name a new beneficiary. All terms of the existing contract continue as before.
2. Receive the death benefit as a lump sum.
3. Elect to annuitize the contract within one year of the date of death.
4. Continue the contract for up to 5 years

Prior to choosing between these four options, it's essential that the spouse understand how the annuity company interprets option #1. This becomes important if the death benefit of the contract is greater than the account value. Usually, this would occur only with a variable annuity, but it can happen with any annuity that has an enhanced death benefit rider. In these cases, the question becomes will the insurance company allow the spouse to continue the contract at the current account value or at the death benefit value? A strict interpretation of the tax code would say that the death benefit is the appropriate value only if the beneficiary elects options 2, 3 or 4. I would argue that under option #1, there is no death benefit. It is merely a continuation of the existing contract. Therefore, the death benefit would not be paid until the second spouse dies. Despite this, many insurance companies do allow the spouse to continue the contract at the death benefit value rather than the account value. They do this in order to hold onto the money. If your contract value is $100,000 and your death benefit is $150,000 and the only way you can get the full $150,000 is to take a lump sum or take it over 5 years, you are going to take the $150,000. This issue can be further complicated by whether or not the contract is owner driven or annuitant driven. If it is annuitant driven but the owner dies, then the tax code will require a death benefit be paid but the death benefit might not be available since the annuitant is still alive. Again, this can vary from company to company depending upon how that company interprets the tax code. ***It is absolutely critical to check on how the insurance company will treat the death benefit and report the taxes before selecting any option.***

Non-Spousal Beneficiary Options:

1. Take a lump sum
2. Annuitize within 12 months of the date of death
3. Continue the contract for up to 5 years

In short, the non-spouse has all of the same options of the spouse with the exception of continuing the contract beyond 5 years. All of these options would be based on the death benefit value rather than the account value. The ability to continue the contract for up to 5 years is designed as a way to allow the beneficiary to spread the taxes out. Prior to selecting this option, verify with the insurance company how they will handle this administratively. Questions to ask include: Can the beneficiary control the investment options? Are there any investment restrictions? Will statements go out to the beneficiary - and if that is the case, how will the death benefit reported? This 5-year rule can be administratively difficult for some insurance companies. They are required to treat the contract as a death claim at the same time they are required to allow the contract to be in force. They also must know when the 5-year limit has been reached. In order to comply with these conflicting requirements, some companies have established administrative rules that may restrict the beneficiary's control of the contract.

Who is responsible for paying the taxes on the death benefit?

While determining the correct tax treatment on annuity income is not always a simple task, determining who should pay the taxes is easy. The person receiving the funds must report all of the tax deferred gain paid out by the death benefit. The income is considered ordinary income and is taxed at the recipient's tax bracket. Since some of today's variable annuities do not have a return of premium death benefits, it is possible for the contract to be worth less at death than it was at the time it was purchased, thereby creating an ordinary income loss for the beneficiary. If this occurs, the beneficiary would be able to report a loss against ordinary income. But even a variable annuity with a return of premium could generate a taxable loss at death. All variable annuities issued since 2004 with a return of premium death benefit, and most issued prior to then, adjust the death benefit pro-rata for any withdrawals. Therefore, a contract that has had withdrawals after the account value has dropped in value could have a death benefit that is less than the original purchase amount. Let's look at an example.

- Client A buys a $100,000 variable annuity with a return of premium death benefit
- Death benefit at time of purchase is therefore $100,000
- Contract drops in value by 30%, leaving an account value of $70,000
- Policy owner withdraws $14,000 (20% of $70,000) from the contract
- Since the death benefit is reduced pro-rata, it drops 20% from $100,000 to $80,000
- Policy owner dies shortly after the withdrawal
- The withdrawal reduced the cost basis on the contract to $86,000 ($100,000 less the $14,000 withdrawal)
- Beneficiary is only entitled to $80,000, thereby creating a $6,000 ordinary income loss

Can you 1035 exchange a death benefit in order to postpone the taxes?

If the beneficiary has no immediate need for the money and doesn't wants to avoid reporting the deferred income, it's not uncommon for her to ask if there is a way to continue to defer the taxes by moving the death benefit into another annuity. Unfortunately, that is not possible. The entire objective of creating the death at distribution rules was to keep people from deferring taxes through multiple generations. Prior to TEFRA people would buy annuities and name their grandchild as the annuitant, thereby allowing them to defer the taxes until the grandchild died. Some companies even allowed you to change the annuitant, thereby effectively allowing for the contract to be tax deferred forever. The U.S Treasury department didn't like that. Therefore, they designed the rules so that the taxes could be deferred only for the lives of the "holder" and his or her spouse.

Bottom line is that if you instruct the insurance company to send the death proceeds directly to another insurance company, expect the original insurance company to send the beneficiary a 1099.

What if a corporation or Trust owns the annuity?

The tax deferral afforded to annuities is only available on contracts owned by individuals. A corporation can own an annuity, but it will receive a 1099 for the income (or loss) each year. A trust can also own an annuity. If that trust is established on behalf of an individual, then that annuity will be tax deferred. Expect the insurance company to request a copy of the trust so that it can determine the appropriate tax treatment. While it's not uncommon to see annuities within trusts, such a structure can create a unique problem at death. Only an individual has the death benefit options listed above. Since a trust is not an individual, the only option upon the death of the annuitant will be a lump sum payable to the Trust.

Tax Treatment of Annuitized Policies

This is covered in sufficient detail in the chapter on immediate annuities. For the purposes of this chapter, I will merely say that when a non-qualified policy is annuitized, each income payment is part principal and part interest based on the life expectancy of the annuitant. The portion of the payment that is non-taxable as a return of premium is called the exclusion allowance and is not taxable. If the annuity payments last long enough to payout all of the cost basis, then 100% of the remaining payments become taxable as long as they continue to be paid.

CHAPTER 8

WHY TAX DEFERRAL IS SO VALUABLE

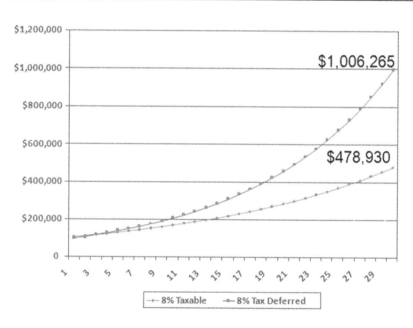

Graphs like the one above are ubiquitous. Financial advisors have used these to demonstrate the power of tax deferred investing – be it through annuities or retirement plans – for as long as I can remember. But my experience is that very few clients really understand why tax deferral is such a valuable tool. Conceptually, everyone understands that it is better to pay taxes later than today, but few can articulate *why*. Let me offer a very simple explanation. When a client buys a taxable investment, you effectively earn two types of interest: interest on the principal, and interest on the interest. When a client buys a tax-deferred investment, however, he or she earns three types of interest: interest on the principal, interest on the interest *and* interest on the money he or she would have paid in taxes each year. The deferred taxes remain in the client's account, free of charge, to earn an additional return. If an investor had to pay taxes each year on his or her earnings, accordingly, the full power of compounding interest would go away.

Yet here is another benefit that is rarely discussed. Whenever I buy a taxable investment, I'm going to get a 1099 each year whether I like it or not. I have no control over when to pay the taxes. Most people will have events in their lives that cause their tax brackets to go up and down. Tax-deferred investments give them control over when to pay the taxes. If they have a year where they are in a relatively high tax bracket, they will have the flexibility to continue the tax deferral. If it's a year when they are in a relatively low tax bracket, then they have the option of taking income in that year, thereby reducing their overall taxation on that particular asset. Tax-deferred annuities give you a level of control over your taxes that you simply cannot get with taxable investments.

Other Benefits of Tax Deferral

1. By turning taxable income into tax deferred income, your clients can potentially reduce other taxes or costs:

2. The 3.8% investment surtax that was created to help pay for the Affordable Care Act is based on an individual's modified adjusted gross income. Income that remains tax deferred is not included in the calculation. By shifting income from taxable to tax deferred, you might be able to reduce or even eliminate this additional tax.

3. Taxes assessed on Social Security is based on adjusted gross income, income from tax-free bonds and ½ of an individual's Social Security benefits. I will also note that the income thresholds for this calculation have not changed since the tax was introduced in 1984. Once again, tax deferred again is not included in this calculation until the money comes out of the annuity.

4. Medicare premiums are based on an individual's reportable income. By utilizing an annuity, you might be able to shift enough taxable income to the tax deferred account to get the client below one of the income thresholds that determine the size of the client's monthly Medicare premium.

Common Criticisms of Deferring Taxes Through the Use of Annuities

Many have argued that the benefits of tax deferral provided by annuities are not sufficient relative to the extra costs of certain annuity products. Because variable annuities are often compared to investments that are taxed at rates other than ordinary income rates, they come up against these criticisms more often than other forms of annuities. So, how true are these arguments? Let's examine them more closely.

1. Fifteen Years Is the Tipping Point

One of the most prevalent arguments is that your client has to hold on to the annuity at least 15 years to realizing the benefits of a tax deferral maneuver. The graph at the beginning of this chapter clearly shows that there is some truth to this argument. While the difference in the account value in year 30 is substantial compared with years, it's not so great after only 10 years and it's almost non-existent before 10 years. And this is assuming an eight percent growth rate. Assume a smaller rate and the time required to begin seeing a difference is even greater. However, this is not an argument against annuities – in general and retirement plans in particular – as much as it is an argument for the need to utilize annuities as part of a long-term investment plan. Unless the inherent investment benefits of the annuity can stack up against other investment options without the benefit of tax deferral, tax deferred annuities (immediate annuities are another story) should not be used as a short-term investment vehicle. But when viewed as part of a long-term plan for retirement, it's hard to beat tax deferral as a means of accumulating money. Don't forget, also, that the client has flexibility to take income along the way that adds additional tax control.

2. Variable annuities turn potential long-term gains into ordinary income

Variable annuities do, indeed, generate ordinary income rather than capital gains, but that does not mean variable annuities are always an inferior investment to mutual funds. When deciding between a mutual fund and a variable annuity, you must consider the client's expected holding period, current tax rate, expected tax rate and trading frequency. First, let's remember that mutual funds have their own potential tax issues. For one thing, it is not uncommon for an investor to inherit unreportable capital gains when purchasing a mutual fund. This can lead to a 1099 even if the investor's fund value had dropped during the year. Secondly, changes in the mutual fund's holdings by the portfolio manager can generate short-term capital gains as well as long-term capital gains. Given that the average holding period of a mutual fund is less than two years, one must ask how many long-term gains that the average investor realizes are actually being realized by the average investor. For an investor who frequently moves money from one fund to another, a variable annuity can be a much more tax-efficient vehicle. Moving money from one sub-account to another within a variable annuity is not a taxable event because the money remains within the tax deferred structure of the annuity. At that point, one must also consider the 3.8 percent investment tax mentioned previously. Increasingly, there is something to be said for not receiving a 1099 for many, many years.

3. Variable annuities do not get a stepped-up cost basis at death.

In addition to being taxed as ordinary income, variable annuities – unlike other securities – do not get a stepped-up cost basis at death. However, given the requirement that mutual fund companies distribute taxable gains each year, one must weigh how much the cost basis will actually step up at death. This tax provision is far more meaningful to individual stocks than mutual funds. Remember, also, that the deferred taxes generated by the annuity are taxed at the beneficiary's tax bracket rather than the owner's. In addition, that beneficiary can choose to spread the taxes out by taking the money over five years – or even longer if he or she elects to annuitize the death benefit (although, I grant you that few choose to do this). However, even if the beneficiary elects to take the money in a lump sum, in my 30-plus years in this business I've never heard of a single beneficiary that complained about the taxes that were due on the money he or she had just inherited.

Key Takeaway

No investor likes to get a 1099 each year. Therefore, deferral can be a wonderful tax management technique. However, when you're trying to decide if tax deferral is a sufficient reason to tip the investment decision in favor of the annuity, you must consider the client's time horizon, current tax bracket and future tax bracket. In general, the longer the time horizon, the higher the current tax bracket and/or the higher the likelihood of a lower tax bracket at retirement, the more powerful the advantage of tax deferral.

CHAPTER 9

HOW A LIVING BENEFIT ON A VARIABLE ANNUITY REALLY WORKS

It is easy to make a living benefit sound magical and wonderful. After all, who wouldn't want a benefit that provides a minimum and known amount of income for life that will not decrease even if the account value goes down and could very well increase if the account value goes up?

Living benefits can indeed be part of the solution to many of your client's retirement income plans, but you must first understand three crucial aspects about how every living benefit works:

1. At its core, a living benefit is just a systematic withdrawal program that the insurance company guarantees for life no matter how the account value performs (assuming, of course, that the policyholder follows all of the rules of the benefit). It's the various rider variations, features and terms that can make this feature seem very complex and mysterious. At the core, however, they are all very simple. The insurance company guarantees that the policyholder can receive a set amount of income every year. This income initially comes out of the policy account value in the form of a systematic withdrawal. If the account value runs out of money before the policyholder dies, the insurance company is required to continue to pay the annual income amount out of its own general account. At the end of the day, this is the guarantee that the policyholder is purchasing.

2. The Income Account is not accessible money. When a client purchases an annuity with a living benefit, the insurance company establishes a second account that I will refer to as the Income Account. It is always nice to see the Income Account increase in value each year, but what really matters is how much actual lifetime income it can support. The highest Income Account does not necessarily translate into the highest lifetime income payments. Although this account does not represent actual accessible funds, every insurance company insists on putting a "$" in front of all Income Account balances on all client statements and in all pieces of literature. In my opinion, this would be like your credit card company putting a "$" sign in front of your points balance. I think it is best to avoid confusion on this matter, so to emphasize that this is not actually money, you will not see a "$" in front of any Income Account example in this book. We will address the intricacies of the Income Account a bit later in this chapter. **Until a policyholder begins to receive the income under the benefit, all he or she really has is a future promise from the insurance company.**

If the policyholder has no intentions of taking lifetime systematic withdrawals from the annuity, he or she should not purchase a living benefit. In fact, if he or she does not plan to begin taking lifetime systematic withdrawals before the age of 75, he or she likely does not need a living benefit. More on that towards the end of this chapter.

Living Benefit Mechanics – the chassis supporting the income guarantee

Despite the fact that every insurance company puts a "$" in front of the value of the Income Account on every client statement and in every client brochure, this account is not money. The Income Account can never be monetized. It can only be used to calculate how much lifetime income that the policy guarantees through the living benefit rider. Since the insurance industry is not big on standardization, there can be many names for this Income Account. The most common ones are "income benefit base," "guaranteed income base," "guaranteed withdrawal account," and "guaranteed Income Account." I will use "Income Account" throughout this book.

The guaranteed growth of the Income Account rewards the policyholder for waiting to receive income by providing more income the longer he or she waits. The tactic is similar to waiting to begin collecting Social Security benefits. The insurance company can benefit from this feature as well. The longer the policyholder waits, the shorter the life expectancy and the fewer years that the insurance company must provide the income. In that sense, the insurance company's risk diminishes. The insurance company's hope is that money will still be in the account on the day the client dies, thereby eliminating the need for the company to ever pay money out of its own reserves.

The initial value of this Income Account is equal to the actual account value at the time the rider is established. I state it this way only because some contracts allow the policyholder to add the rider after the policy is issued. Obviously, this doesn't happen often, so for all practical purposes the initial value of the Income Account is the amount invested in the annuity. Typically, the insurance company guarantees to grow this Income Account by a specific percentage rate each year for ten years or until "income" is taken from the account, whichever comes first. It's very important to understand that the vast majority of all insurance companies define taking "income" as making a single withdrawal for any reason whatsoever. Therefore, if the plan is to grow the guaranteed income for down the road, the annuity should be the last place your client goes to meet any liquidity needs. Five percent is a very common guaranteed growth rate on the Income Account, but on indexed annuities it can be as high as eight percent. This growth rate is guaranteed even if the account value decreases.

Variations of this part of the process do exist. Let's review the most common ones that you are likely to encounter:

1. The growth rate could be either a simple interest rate or a compounded rate. For example, if the growth rate is a simple 5 percent, then the insurance company will add only 5,000 each and every year on a 100,000 initial Income Account balance. If the growth rate were five percent compounded, however, the insurance company would add 5,000 in year one: 5,250 in year in year two, etc. Not surprisingly, the higher the stated guaranteed growth rate, the more likely the insurance company will use simple interest to calculate the accumulation, rather than compounded interest. A growth rate of 8 percent can sound great, but this is the equivalent of less than 7 percent compounded if the client plans on waiting 10 years to begin receiving income.

2. Most companies will guarantee this growth rate for 10 years. Living benefit designs prior to 2011 typically started this 10-year-period over anytime there is a "step up" of the Income Account value (we will discuss how "step ups" work later). On variable annuities, that's a rare feature today. This means that a living benefit works best for a policyholder who intends to start the lifetime income within 10 years after the date he or she purchases the annuity. If the client has a time frame longer than 10 years, you will likely need to turn to an indexed annuity in order to find a living benefit that will increase the Income Account for more than that time period. If you can't find one, make sure the client understands that he or she should not expect an increase in the guaranteed income amount once they reach the 10-year policy anniversary.

3. Contracts sold prior to 2011 often guaranteed that the value of the Income Account would automatically double on the 10th anniversary, *provided the policyholder made no withdrawals of any kind* **during that 10-year period**. No company offers this feature today, although one guarantees to double the Income Account by the later of age 70, or 12 years after the policy issue date. Policies that have this feature can be very valuable. By now, most of the policies with this feature will have reached the ten-year anniversary and therefore would have already experienced the doubling of the Income Account. However, if you have one that has not yet reached that magic mark, make sure the policyholder does not take a withdrawal prior to the tenth anniversary.

"Stepping Up" the Income Account

We have established that a policy's account value and Income Account are not equal; but the former does influence the latter. The vast majority of the living benefit designs periodically compare the account value to the Income Account. This is typically done on every policy anniversary. If the account value is higher than the Income Account, then the Income Account is increased – or "stepped up" – to the account value. Essentially, the relationship between the account value and the Income Account starts all over again on any step up. This includes the fees as well. The terms of the benefit give the insurance company the ability to increase the rider fee upon any step up. Given the change in the cost of these riders over the last five years, this fee increase can be substantial – perhaps as much as one full percentage point per year. Of course, there are variations of this feature as well.

1. Older designs typically restart the 10-year guarantee period for increasing the Income Account. If a step up occurs on the fifth policy anniversary, the policyholder will be guaranteed that the Income

Account will increase at the minimum rate at least until the fifteenth policy anniversary. Very few of today's contracts offer this very valuable feature.

2. Some contracts consider the account value on more than just the anniversary date. While they typically still step up only on the policy anniversary, they use the highest value from the preceding quarter or monthly. For example, if the contract has an anniversary date of January 1, a quarterly step-up contract would look at the contract value as of the previous April 1, July 1 or October 1 as well as the value on January 1. The highest of the four dates would be used to determine if a step up has occurred. The same would be true with a contract that looks at each monthly value. These designs improve the odds of getting a step up because they capture values throughout the policy year. This partially protects the policyholder from a significant drop in the account value just prior to the policy anniversary. Certainly, a policyholder with a policy anniversary back on June 1, 2008 would have appreciated locking in some of the market gains before the market started to fall in late 2007.

3. Some designs offer a living benefit that steps up daily. Prudential Life Insurance Company originated this concept. Unlike the other designs, it does not limit step ups only on the policy anniversary dates. It literally can adjust up each and every day the market is open. Each day, the insurance company will compare the account value to the Income Account. On any day the account value is higher than the current Income Account, the Income Account will be stepped up to that day's account value. This allows the policyholder to immediately capture any market increases. To gain this feature, the policyholder must allow the account value to be controlled by a formula proprietary to the insurance company. For example, Prudential uses an investment algorithm that systematically moves money to a bond account if the account value gets too far below the Income Account. The algorithm will move the money back only as the account value begins to grow faster than the Income Account. With these designs, it should be noted that given today's low interest rates, if a drop in the market causes the algorithm to move a significant percentage of the account value into a fixed Income Account, it is very possible that the account value will never experience enough growth to have money moved back into equities.

How are Fees Calculated on a Living Benefit?

It was Benjamin Franklin who said, "In this world nothing can be said to be certain, except death and taxes." In the complex world of annuities, fees are a certainty. There are some older contracts that calculated the living benefit fees on the account value. However, prior to the financial crisis of 2007-2008 the insurance companies that had such a methodology began to calculate the fees on the Income Account value and then deduct them from the account value. Since the Income Account is rarely less than the account value, this design allows the insurance company to capture more fee income, which in turn allows them to guarantee higher growth on the Income Account. Since policyholders seemed to be more concerned with the growth in the

Income Account than the cost of the rider – especially before the financial crisis – this was a tradeoff that seemed to satisfy everyone.

By calculating the fee on the Income Account rather than the account value, the insurance company can essentially take a fee that is greater than it can appear on the surface. For example, if the rider fee is one percent of the Income Account and the Income Account is 100,000, the total fee is $1,000 for the year. Remember though that since the Income Account is not money, this fee is actually deducted from the account value. Therefore, if the account value is only $80,000, then the one percent fee on the Income Account is actually 1.25 percent of the account value. This fee methodology also allows the insurance company to essentially charge the policyholder more as the difference between the Income Account and the account value widens. Of course, it also hastens the liquidation of the account value; which is something the insurance company does not want to have happen. Therefore, the design is a bit of a two-way street for the insurance company.

How Does The Practice of "Stacking" Affect the Annuity Structure?

The term 'stacking' admittedly doesn't sound technical enough to describe an important financial concept in a discussion about annuities. Let me begin by describing what 'stacking' actually involves. Stacking concerns how the guaranteed growth rate of the Income Account is calculated after a step up. If the contract "stacks", then the guaranteed growth rate is applied to the new, higher Income Account value.

Virtually every living benefit "stacks" when a step up occurs. However, there are some that do not stack, therefore it's necessary to include a section on stacking and why it's important.

For example, on a living benefit that "stacks" if the Income Account steps up from 125,000 to 150,000, then the five percent guaranteed growth rate is now credited on the 150,000 Income Account value. If a contract doesn't stack, then guaranteed growth rate is not applied to the stepped-up amount. For a contract that does not stack, when a step up occurs due to the account value exceeding the Income Account, the insurance company essentially creates a second Income Account. One Income Account is the original premium growing at the guaranteed growth rate each and every year. This account is not influenced in any way by the account value. The second Income Account is essentially the highest policy anniversary value. To determine the amount of guaranteed income, the insurance company takes the higher of these two Income Account values.

Graphically, these concepts would appear as follows:

Stacking vs. No Stacking - 5% Deferral Bonus (1997-20013)

Assumes no withdrawals during the first 10 years – withdrawals will affect the deferral bonus credit.

This is a hypothetical situation for two policies purchased in 1997 – one that stacks and one that does not. For simplicity purposes, we will assume they both have identical performance represented by the "account value" line.

The account value fluctuates over time. The strong performance in the first three years of the contract caused step ups in both product designs on each of the first three policy anniversaries. The tech crash causes the value to fall back to almost the initial investment of $100,000 by then end of 2002, rising back to almost $180,000 prior to the financial crises of 2007-09 and then falling back to almost $100,000 in 2009. It's not until 2013 that the account value exceeds the high it reached in

1999. The Income Account for the policy that doesn't stack is the greater of the two values – one that grows at 5% each year for the first 10 years (represented by the "deferral bonus – no stacking line") and one that steps up each time the account value exceeds it, but then stays flat until the next step up (represented by the "2nd account – not stacking line"). By comparison, the policy that stacks steps up each of the first three years like the non-stacking line, but then continues to grow at 5% each year until the later of 10 years or the next step up. This is represented by the "5% deferral bonus line". It's clear to see why the stacking method can lead to a significantly higher Income Account (and therefore income) than the non-stacking policy when the policy experiences a significant decline in the account value. The policy that stacks ends up with an Income Account of 290,200, thereby providing an income of $14,510 for life if we assume a five percent payout. The policy that doesn't stack has an Income Account of only 193,470, thereby providing an income for life of only $9,902.

Clearly, a stacking design is a much superior choice. A design that doesn't stack compares favorably to a stacking design only when the account value performs well and step ups regularly occur. In this scenario, the account value is continually growing faster than the guaranteed growth rate on the income account, which essentially negates the benefits of the guaranteed growth rate. Of course, this is not the market scenario against which living benefits are designed to protect. The goal is to provide as much income as possible in the event the market underperforms. Only a stacking design will provide growth of the Income Account during a market correction that occurs after a step up captures an account value peak.

How Likely Are Step Ups and Are They Always Ripe for Picking?

From a practical standpoint, step-ups are most likely to occur in the first few years of the contract. If the account value falls too far behind the Income Account, the guaranteed growth ·of the Income Account combined with the fees of the rider and any account value withdrawals make it unlikely that the account value will ever exceed the Income Account. This is particularly true if the rider comes with severe investment restrictions. But should a policyholder always accept a step up? This was never a question when these riders first to the market. A step up means more guaranteed income, and who wouldn't want more guaranteed income? However, with today's pricing, the answer to this question is not nearly as certain.

Let's say, for example, that your client, whom we will call Mark, has a contract with an account value of $200,000 and an Income Account of 180,000 as of a step up date. Let's further assume that the rider gives Mark five percent of the Income Account for life. The insurance company informs him that he is eligible for a step up, and that the rider fee will increase from 0.60 percent to 1.2 percent. Should Mark do the step up? Not before running the calculations of two different scenarios:

1. If the step up *is not* taken:
Lifetime income: 180,000 x .05 = $9,000 per year
Annual rider fee: 180,000 x .006 = $1,080

2. If step up *is* taken:

New lifetime income: 200,000 x .05 = $10,000 (an increase of $1,000 per year for life)

New annual rider cost: 200,000 x .012 = $2,400 (an increase of $1,320 per year)

So, what's the proper answer? It depends. If Mark is only concerned about the highest possible lifetime income, then the fees are secondary. Yes, he is paying $1,320 per year more to get an additional $1,000 in lifetime income, but once the income begins, the account value – and therefore the fees – is almost irrelevant. If what he really wants and needs is $10,000 per year for life, then if the account value falls to zero faster due to higher fees should not matter. However, the answer becomes more complicated if he is not sure if and when he is going to begin receiving the income (although if Mark doesn't plan on ever needing the income, I have to wonder why a client like him has the rider at all).

Other things clients should consider when trying to decide whether or not to step up an annuity contract:

1. If a client decides not to step up the contract, will they still have the option to do so in future years? Some contracts, particularly older ones, give clients the option of stepping up on any policy anniversary. With such contracts a client could push off the fee increase and still potentially lock in higher guaranteed income. Using our example above, the client could elect to not step up the contract, thereby keeping the fee at 0.6 percent with the hopes of having an account value equal to or greater than $200,000 on a future date. Of course, if the market drags the account value down, this strategy can backfire on the client spectacularly. In addition, many contracts issued today offer a "use it or lose it" option on step ups. With these designs, if the client elects not to accept a step up, he or she would give up the right to any future step ups.

2. Are there are any other consequences of a step up? Step ups are not always free – of consequences, that is. An increasing number of contracts limit the investment options, or force further asset allocation restrictions if a client accepts a step-up feature on the contract. If this is the case, your client might end up sacrificing future performance while attempting to secure an increased guaranteed income.

3. Are there consequences of *not* stepping up the account? Some contracts issued today actually reduce the income guarantee on the contracts if the client doesn't accept the fee increase that comes with the step up. Insurance companies do this in order to force a fee increase upon the client. Personally, I think this is a horrible product design. While the goal is to get as many step ups as possible in order to get higher income guarantees, I don't believe the policyholder should be penalized should they decline the fee increase that comes with the step up. You must make your clients fully aware of this particular design twist.

Receiving Income

Ensuring the flow of guaranteed income is the whole point of annuity contracts, so it is tempting to choose a living benefit rider that favors the greatest growth in the contract's Income Account. But always remember: the Income Account is *not usable money*. It is merely a number that providers use to calculate how much lifetime income the policyholder can receive. Both you and your clients will much better off focusing on the income. An extra 0.5 percent income rate may not sound like much, but the math would indicate that it could be far more meaningful than an additional growth rate of one percent on the Income Account. Let's just look at a simple example:

Policy #1: A $100,000 policy offers a six percent guaranteed growth rate in the Income Account (simple interest), and 4.5 percent rate income rate for life. The client plans to begin drawing down income in 10 years.

Guaranteed value of the Income Account in 10 years at a six percent simple interest: 160,000

Guaranteed level of income: 160,000 x .045 = $7,200

Policy #2: A $100,000 policy with a five percent guaranteed growth rate in the Income Account (simple interest), and five percent for life. Similar to the previous example, the client plans to begin income in 10 years.

Guaranteed value of Income Account in 10 years at five percent simple interest: 150,000

Guaranteed level of income: 150,000 x .05 = $7,500

While the Income Account on Policy #2 only increased 50% from 100,000 to 150,000 versus a 60% growth rate for Policy #1 (100,000 to 160,000), Policy #2 guaranteed $300 more in income than Policy #s1. The bottom line is that while both the growth rate and the income rate are important, you should always look first for the highest possible income rate.

How to Measure a Compounded Growth Rate Against a Simple Interest

We are all familiar with the power of compounded interest over simple interest – both as individual investors and advisors helping others manage their investments. This example is also helpful when demonstrating the additional value of a compounded growth over simple interest, on the Income Account. Let's go in for a look from a different angle.

<u>Policy #1</u> grows at a six percent compounded interest, creating an Income Account of 179,085 on a $100,000 investment after 10 years, which would then generate $8,954 in annual income – assuming a 5% withdrawal rate.

<u>Policy #2</u> grows at seven percent simple interest, creating an Income Account of 170,000, which would generate $8,500 in annual income. While seven percent may sound much better than six percent, it doesn't take long for the power of compounding to more than make up the difference. The bottom line is, always focus on the amount of guaranteed income, not the size of the Income Account.

Originally, most of the living benefit designs used a compounded rate of growth on the Income Account to calculate the amount of the income guarantee. Today, such designs are in the minority. Insurance companies have learned that many advisors and their clients do not differentiate between the five percent-compounded rate and the five percent simple rate. The focus is typically on the five percent, not the method of calculation. And don't look for the marketing material to highlight this distinction – particularly if the insurance company uses a simple rate of interest. Switching from a compounded rate of interest to a simple rate became an easy way for insurance companies to quietly reduce the guaranteed benefit.

How a Step up Impacts the Income

The Income Account is not the only element of a living benefit contract that affects a policy's guaranteed lifetime income. You might recall that any step up will increase a policy's guaranteed lifetime income. It can also impact the value of the growth rate in the Income Account. Remember, a step up essentially resets the terms of the rider. The Income Account is stepped up to the new account value and the fee structure changes to reflect the insurance company's current pricing assumptions. This also means that any advantage one rider design has over another when it comes to the guaranteed growth rate of the Income Account, can be cancelled out entirely. For example, let's assume that Company A guarantees to grow the Income Account value at five percent and Company B grows its Income Account at seven percent. Let's further assume that the account values experience the same level of growth, therefore both riders step up after year one. When the step up occurs, the Income Account growth advantage of Rider B vs. Rider A is completely negated. This is shown graphically below:

5% deferral bonus GMWB vs. 7% deferral bonus

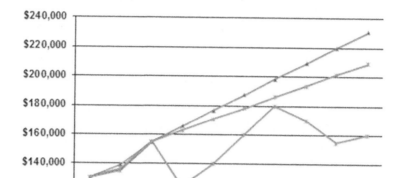

Again, for simplicity purposes, we assume the account value is the same for both policies. Since the account value grows faster than the Income Account in each of the first three years, both policies get step ups equaling the account value. It didn't matter if the whether the rider credited a 5% or 7% bonus to the Income Account. However, when the account value falls in year 4, the Income Account begins to grow at the bonus rate. Here is where the 7% bonus begins to pay off in terms of a higher Income Account.

The message here is that while the guaranteed growth rate of the Income Account is important and should be considered, it is not as important as many think. Four key factors drive the amount of income a rider will ultimately provide, and here is how I rank them, in order of importance:

1. The growth rate of the underlying account value. Nothing will increase the income faster than an account value that grows. Therefore, you should always look for a rider design that gives you the greatest investment flexibility.

2. The payout rate on the Income Account. As nice as it is to see the Income Account grow faster, the size of the payout rate is much more important. For example, a rider with a five percent payout must have an income account that is 20% higher than a similar product with a six percent payout.

3. The guaranteed growth rate of the Income Account.

4. The rider fees. One might wonder why I listed the fees last. The larger the fee drag, the harder the underlying investments must work in order for the account value to grow enough to provide step ups. However, the primary purpose of the rider is to fill an expected future income need. The fees might keep the account holder from getting future step ups, but they don't impact the contract's underlying income guarantee.

Who should buy a living benefit?

A living benefit might sound like a uniformly worthwhile component to add to any annuity contract, but they are not for every client and situation. Only clients who expect to have an income need in retirement should consider the living benefit. In today's interest rate environment, living benefits are not cheap. No matter if you add one to a variable annuity or an indexed annuity, the fees and the corresponding investment restrictions (on variable annuities) will create a tremendous drag on the potential account value growth. If the client does not expect to have an income need, then he or she is essentially paying for unnecessary insurance.

Approximately, four out of five variable annuities sold today have a living benefit. I can't help but wonder if the benefit was appropriately recommended as a future income source in all of those situations. Prior to the financial crisis of 2007-2008, living benefits could be purchased with mild investment restrictions. Living benefits were often added to these contracts as a form of portfolio insurance. "You probably won't need this, but just in case a severe market decline causes your account value to drop significantly, we can recover your investment through the living benefit," was a common approach. Given the limited investment restrictions and lower rider fees, this approach was completely understandable. Today's operating environment is a far cry from that period. With one notable exception, every variable annuity either places severe restrictions on any equity allocation or requires the policyholder to invest in a volatility-managed sub-account. Either way, a policyholder is unlikely to have more than a 70 percent allocation to equities if a living benefit is added. Therefore, if the client's primary objective is account value growth and the income need is unknown at the time of purchase, a living benefit should not be added to the contract. Why allow the living benefit's attendant investment restrictions to severely limit the growth of the contract value if income is not a primary goal?

A Living Benefit's Impact on a Variable Annuity vs. an Indexed Annuity

Insurance companies offer a wide array of annuity products, but variable and indexed annuities are generally the two main underlying chassis on which all products are built. As your clients' advisor, you will need to help them weigh various factors before choosing between the two basic frameworks. When considering whether to add the living benefit rider, the client's income need should be at the forefront. An indexed annuity company does not have to worry about the markets causing a drop in the account value, so they will always be able to provide more initial guaranteed income than a variable annuity company. However, since the cap rates on today's index annuities are typically several percentage points less than the guaranteed increases in the Income Account, it is highly unlikely that an indexed annuity policyholder will ever get a step up. Therefore, the initial income guarantees are likely to never increase. Whatever amount of income is guaranteed on the 10th policy anniversary when the policy is issued is indeed going to be the guarantee when the policy reaches year 10 (assuming no withdrawals or additions to the policy). Simply put, the initial guaranteed income on an indexed annuity with a living benefit is the most the client should ever expect to receive.

A variable annuity, however, can get a step up in the income base. Therefore, one can look at the amount of income that is initially guaranteed on a variable annuity with a living benefit as the least the client should expect to receive. Any step up will subsequently increase the amount of expected income. A variable annuity will provide less guaranteed income initially than an indexed annuity, but *if* the initial difference is not considerable and *if* the client expects the growth in the Income Account value to increase the amount of income, then the variable annuity could be a better choice.

And yet there is another important consideration. What are the odds of your clients getting a step up? Given today's interest rates, a required fixed income allocation of 30 percent or more combined with the contract fees and the rider fees means that a policyholder will likely need to experience equity returns of at least 10 percent in the first couple of years in order to get an increase in guaranteed income as a result of a step up. This is particularly true if the policyholder is required to utilize a volatility-managed account. For the most part, these accounts have severely underperformed the market to date. If a contract goes several years without a step up, thereby creating a larger gap between the actual account value and the Income Account, equity returns of close to 20 percent might be necessary in order to get an increase in the guaranteed income level!

Given today's pricing and investment restrictions, I strongly caution any advisor against overselling the possibility of getting more income than originally guaranteed at the time the contract is issued. Step ups have occurred before, and they will again. However, it's likely to happen only if the equity markets perform well in the first couple of years of the policy. If the early performance on a variable annuity causes the account value to fall significantly short of the Income Account, the fee drags and investment restrictions are going to make step ups unlikely. It is essential, therefore, that the policyholder understand that the living benefit's purpose is to provide a specific level of income at an expected time in the future. If you and your client cannot articulate how much that income need is and when it might be needed in the future, think twice about adding a living benefit and saddling the contract with the rider's inherent investment restrictions.

When Adding a Living Benefit on a Variable Annuity Invest Aggressively

We have discussed the basic function of a living benefit rider – to insure future guaranteed income against market-driven declines in account values. Why create that extra layer of protection by investing the funds conservatively? Yes, your compliance department might flag an aggressive investment strategy on an account without an aggressive profile. Also, you must assess your client's risk tolerance: Does he or she have the fortitude to withstand severe market swings that will affect the annuity's underlying market value? As a portfolio strategy, however, the variable annuity should contain some of the client's most aggressive account allocations because of the addition of the living benefit. After all, the living benefit is essentially insurance that protects the client's future income if the account value does not perform as expected. What better asset to take additional equity exposure than an insured asset?

If you buy into this philosophy, then investors should steer clear of any variable annuity that significantly restricts equity exposure. Essentially, such product designs require the policyholder to not only pay the rider fee to cover the cost of the income insurance, but also pay for some of the insurance company's hedging costs by giving up investment flexibility. My advice on using living benefits on today's variable annuities is simple:

1. Make sure the guaranteed income is part of a carefully deliberated income plan. If the client doesn't know if he or she will need the variable annuity for income, don't limit its returns by adding a living benefit.
2. Invest the money as aggressively as your compliance department will allow. You will know, from day one, the minimum amount of income your client will get. A heavy allocation to equities gives your client the best chance of getting more income than the original guarantee.

CHAPTER 10
LIVING BENEFITS ON INDEXED ANNUITIES

Having tackled the complexities of the best investment approach on the living benefit rider and how the feature works in a volatility-managed sub-account, you might wonder how the living benefit impacts indexed annuities. I am glad you asked. People who plan to draw down on the income in their mid-60's are the sweet spot for living benefits on indexed annuities. If you run an illustration on a 55-year-old who begins the income at age 65, most reasonable return assumptions will show that the account value on most indexed annuity designs would be completely depleted when the client reaches his or her early 80's. At that point, the insurance company would be exposed to high longevity risk, and be obligated to continue funding the guaranteed income for the rest of the person's life. One doesn't have to be an actuarial wiz to realize that under such a scenario, the indexed annuity not only fills an income need, but also provides an outstanding long-term return to the client.

Regardless of when the living benefit is purchased, if the client does not elect to begin receiving the income prior to the age of 75, it is highly likely that the rider would be needed (or perhaps wasn't needed in the first place).

Let's illustrate this through the example of a 75-year-old whom we'll call Policyholder A. This client owns an indexed annuity with a living benefit that has an account value of $100,000 and an Income Account of 125,000. Due to this client's age the living benefit allows him to take 6.5 percent, $8,125 to be exact, of the income base for life. Now let's assume that the account value earns three percent per year on average net of the rider fees.

Quick quiz! At what age would Policyholder A run out of money, thereby making it necessary for the insurance company to begin making payments?

Answer: Policyholder A would run out of money in the 17th policy year at the ripe old age of 92. Would the client need the living benefit? As one of my colleagues likes to ask, 'How likely is it your client is still alive at age 92? And how important is it that you protect against the possibility that he lives well beyond his life expectancy?'

With each year beyond age 75, that Policyholder A delays taking the income, the need for the living benefit diminishes. At some point, funding that extra layer of insurance becomes silly. In fact, if an indexed annuity company is allowing its professionals to sell living benefits riders to 80-year-old clients, I would argue that they are not meeting their responsibility to ensure the suitability of the purchase.

Let's examine Policyholder B now. She too bought an indexed annuity, but skipped the living benefit. Let us also to assume that her account value is $110,000 because she never had the living benefit fee deducted from her account value during the accumulation phase. We will also assume that her account earns on average 3.75 percent per year because there is no living benefit rider.

Like Policyholder A, she takes $8,125 out of the policy each year. At what age would she run out of income? The math tells us that she runs out of money at age 96, twenty-one years after the income starts. So, let's ask again, 'Is she likely to still be alive?' More importantly, does someone who is not likely to run out of money until the age of 96 need to pay for a living benefit to guarantee against either living past that age?

CHAPTER 11

PRO TIPS ON LIVING BENEFITS – CRUCIAL INFORMATION YOU MAY OR MAY NOT HAVE BEEN TOLD

If you think helping your clients assemble smooth retirement strategies is complicated, consider the task facing the insurance companies. A single miscalculation or faulty assumption could result in an expensive mistake. In an attempt to reduce the uncertainty, these riders come with many rules and restrictions. Although these provisions are critical to understanding and implementing living benefit riders to bump up their suitability for your clients, insurance companies are not always proactive about alerting policyholders about these myriad rules. In addition, many of the specifics are often disclosed in documentation that policyholders seldom examine closely, like contract footnotes and the prospectus. Despite these hurdles to educating advisors and policyholders about the details underpinning living benefits riders, you must understand how they work. One crucial mistake can deprive a policyholder of the optimal lifetime income that best suits their needs. This chapter will help you navigate these rules – many of which are fully explained only in prospectuses that can be hundreds of pages long.

1. Excess Withdrawals

One of the most common snafus you are likely to see unfold on annuities with living benefits stems from excess withdrawals of which occur inadvertently. As an example, a simple phone call to the insurance company asking how much the policyholder can take out at "no cost" can lead to the technically correct answer of "10 percent of the account value." While clients might be able to withdraw that 10 percent without a surrender charge, the proceeds will likely be more than the amount allowed under any living benefit rider, in essence creating an excess withdrawal.

The insurance company's marketing literature will typically include a comment that reads something like, "An excess withdrawal may lead to lower lifetime income payments." This is technically accurate, but it is also a form of soft-pedaling. It is more accurate to replace the word "may" with the words, "will almost certainly." Unless the account value is significantly less than the value of the income account at the time of the withdrawal, any excess withdrawal will reduce the policyholder's future income payments. The only question that remains is 'how much will the allowable income be reduced?' The amount of the income adjustment depends on the type of design the insurance company built into the product. The following three methods are the most common. I list them in order of severity, from the least to the greatest.

a. Income Account Reduced Pro-rata by the Excess Amount of the Withdrawal

With this method, the account value is first reduced by the amount of the allowable withdrawal under the rider. It is then reduced pro-rata by the excess withdrawal amount, or the amount taken that what is contractually allowable. The excess withdrawal reduces the Income Account; therefore, the policyholder will experience a reduction in future income payments allowed by the rider. Let's examine an illustration of this.

Account Value: $80,000

Income Account: 110,000

Five percent GMWB withdrawal allowed: $5,500

Actual withdrawal taken: $7,500

Excess Withdrawal Amount: $2,000

Account Value after allowed five percent withdrawal: $80,000 - $5,500 = $74,500

Percentage reduction in account value due to excess: $2,000/$74,500 = 2.7 percent

Reduction in Income Account: 110,000 x (1-.027) = 107,300

New five percent GMWB withdrawal amount: $5,351

As you can see, the $2,000 excess withdrawal costs the policyholder $149 in future annual income payments. Instead of being able to take $5,500 per year for life, the new adjusted allowable amount is $5,351.

b. The income Account reduced pro-rata by the entire amount of the withdrawal

With this method, the policyholder does not get any credit for the amount of the allowable withdrawal.

Account Value: $80,000

Income Account: 110,000

Five percent GMWB withdrawal allowed: $5,500

Actual withdrawal taken: $7,500

Excess Withdrawal Amount: $2,000

Account Value after withdrawal: $80,000 - $7,500 = $72,500

Percent reduction in account value due to withdrawal: $7,500/$80,000 = 9.4 percent

Reduction in Income Account: 110,000 x (1-.094) = 99,687

New five percent GMWB withdrawal amount: $4,984

The account value is reduced by 9.4 percent; the Income Account is also reduced by the same percentage. As you can see, in this case, the $2,000 excess withdrawal leads to a $516 reduction in any future annual income payments.

c. The Reduced Income Account matches the account value

Early living benefit designs essentially reset the Income Account to the account value on any excess withdrawal. This method is the most precarious of them all for two reasons: it could wipe out any increases in the Income Account prior to the withdrawal, and it can reduce the annual income payments to an amount less than originally promised when the rider was purchased.

Account Value: $80,000

Income Account: 110,000

5% GMWB withdrawal allowed: $5,500

Actual withdrawal taken: $7,500

Excess Withdrawal Amount: $2,000

Account Value after withdrawal: $80,000 - $7,500 = $72,500

New Income Account: 72,500

New five percent GMWB withdrawal amount: $3,625

You can clearly see the cost in the form of lost income that can occur as a result of this method. By taking just $2,000 too much, the policyholder has reduced the amount of future income payments by $1,875 per year. Obviously, the policyholder would be better off getting the extra $2,000 in cash from virtually any other source. Fortunately, most insurance companies that used this method of calculating excess withdrawals changed to one of the prior two methods beginning in 2006.

2. The Definition of "Income" Under the Terms of the Benefit

Insurance companies that offer complex products like annuities must explain every concept with crystal clarity. So how do they define "income?" The client literature will commonly say that the Income Account is guaranteed to grow by a certain percentage each year **"until income payments begin."** But what is the definition of income payments? Most policyholders would likely say that income payments don't begin until they begin to regularly receive the guaranteed lifetime income according to a pre-determined interval (annually, quarterly or monthly). Unfortunately, for most rider structures such an assumption would be incorrect. Under the terms of the living benefit, as soon as the policyholder takes a single withdrawal, he or she has been deemed to be taking "income payments" (Note – some contracts allow the policyholder to take one withdrawal without beginning regular income payments).

Just one withdrawal, depending on the terms of the contract, can inadvertently halt the annual guaranteed growth of the Income Account simply by taking a single withdrawal. In addition, it's not difficult to see how this withdrawal could also be treated as an excess withdrawal. Let's go back to the inadvertent excess withdrawal example that I cited previously. If the policyholder calls the insurance company and requests a withdrawal equal to the annual free withdrawal, the insurance company could easily tell the policyholder that he or she could take as much as ten percent of the account value. Beware the caveat, however, because the transaction would create an excess withdrawal and cause the contract to stop crediting the five- to eight percent annual growth rate of the income account. Hopefully, the service representative would explain to the policyholder that, "while your contract allows you to take 10 percent of your account value without a surrender charge, you are only allowed 5% of your Income Account. Such a withdrawal would create a reduction in your future income payments. In addition, we will stop crediting you the five percent growth rate on your Income Account." What are the chances of the insurance company representative giving that complete of an answer?

Unless you want to count on the insurance company representative making that full disclosure, it is my recommendation that you instruct the policyholder to let you know if he or she intends to take any money out of an annuity with a living benefit. This is especially true for living benefits on annuities in custodial individual retirement accounts.

3. Watch Out For Living Benefits On Policies in Custodial IRA Accounts

All custodial IRA accounts are going to have an annual fee charged to the account. If the annuity is the only asset in the account, that fee has to come from somewhere. If that fee is taken from the annuity, and the insurance company deems that withdrawal to be "income" under the terms of the rider, the custodian will inadvertently stop any future guaranteed growth of the Income Account. In addition, if the policyholder has already taken the allowable annual amount under the living benefit, that simple, small custodial fee could create an excess withdrawal.

4. When Should Income Payments Begin?

While the insurance company brochure will likely show case studies of policyholders that begin income payments at age 65 or 70, you will never see anything that will guide you as to the optimum time to begin income payments. Undoubtedly, the insurance company will say that it is not its role to provide "investment advice" and therefore it would be inappropriate for the company to suggest a policyholder should or shouldn't begin taking income payments. While this may be true, it's also true that the insurance company does not want the policyholder to begin taking income payments. Why do you think living benefits guarantee an annual growth rate in the Income Account? This provision encourages the policyholder not to begin income payments. As outlined in the previous chapter on living benefits, the longer a policyholder waits to begin taking income payments, the lower the probability that the policyholder liquidates the account value before he or she dies. As long as there is even $1 in the account value when the rider is terminated – either through death or surrender - the insurance company essentially charges fees each year for a benefit that was completely covered by the policyholder's own money. For this reason, income payments on variable annuities should begin no later than age 75. At age 75, the remaining life expectancy is about 14 years for a male and 16 years for a female. Unless the income base is significantly higher than the account value, it is unlikely that even a lifetime withdrawal of five- to six-percent lifetime withdrawals would liquidate the account value before a person of that age dies.

When adding a living benefit onto an indexed annuity, it might be a good idea to target an income start date of no later than age 72. Since the account value of an indexed annuity can never go down in value in any given year, a policy is not likely to ever get to a point where the Income Account will far exceed the account value. Therefore, it will typically take longer for a five percent or six percent systematic withdrawal from an indexed annuity to fully liquidate the account value.

The bottom line is that the older the policyholder gets, the less likely it will be that the guaranteed income received under the living benefit will liquidate the account value before the policyholder dies. Therefore, *there is* an age at which every policyholder should either turn on the income or drop the rider.

Now that we have established that income should begin at no later than age 72, let's examine the circumstances under which the guaranteed income should begin. The answer is really quite simple: Income payments should begin when the policyholder needs more retirement income. When that date arrives, your client is going to ask your opinion on how the additional income should be created. Your first instinct may be to suggest taking it from the client's IRA, setting up a systematic withdrawal plan, or structuring up a bond ladder portfolio. There is a tendency to want to continue to defer the annuity knowing that each year you wait will mean more income. I would suggest that this is the wrong conclusion. The client bought the annuity with the living benefit to provide lifetime income, so it is better to use it for the purpose for which it was purchased. Also, since you know it will provide a specific level of income for life no matter how the underlying asset performs, you can invest the rest of the client's portfolio more aggressively.

This advice carries some exceptions. First, all riders require the policyholder to be a certain age in order to guarantee the income for life. In today's market, that is typically when a policyholder turns 65. For older contracts, it can be as young as 59 ½. So, make sure the client meets the age requirements. Second, many living benefit designs have a higher income payout at certain ages. For example, it may pay five percent at age 65, 5.5 percent at age 70 and 6 percent at age 75. Similarly, older living benefit designs often guaranteed to double the Income Account on the 10th or 12th policy anniversary (if no withdrawals were previously made). If the client is just a year or two away from a new age range or a doubling of the Income Account, it may make sense to defer taking the income until that date.

A special note about taking income from indexed annuities with living benefits

Many indexed annuity companies seem to be basing their living benefit pricing on the assumption that many of the policyholders will not turn on the income until they are well into their 70's or 80's – if they turn it on at all. If you run an illustration of a 55-year-old that buys an indexed annuity with a living benefit and then turns on the income at age 65, unless you assume superior account value performance, you will likely find that the account value will be exhausted when the client is in his or her early 80's. The insurance company would be on the hook for continuing the income payments for 10-15 years. In fact, the guaranteed income in this scenario could outstrip a deferred income annuity that also begins lifetime income at age 65 – despite the fact that the indexed annuity offers both liquidity and a potential death benefit to the beneficiary and the deferred income annuity does not!

How could your client get to that outcome? For starters, when someone buys a deferred income annuity, the insurance company must assume that every policyholder that is still alive at the income start date will indeed begin to receive the income. Given the lack of liquidity in most of these products, the company must assume a zero percent lapse rate. This is not the case with the indexed annuity. The company will assume that a certain percentage of the policyholders will surrender the contract before the account value goes to zero. They will further assume that a certain percentage of the policyholders will never start receiving income even if they keep the policy. All of these assumptions give them the flexibility to increase the allowable guaranteed income for those that actually use the rider as it was designed. The bottom line: When an indexed annuity is used as part of a strategic retirement income plan, your clients can benefit from the policyholders that do not efficiently use the rider.

An Uncommon, but Important, Question: What If My Client Doesn't Need Additional Income ... and Maybe Never Will?

We have laid out several longevity risk management strategies to suit a range of circumstances – except one. This situation that rarely develops, but still needs to be tackled: What to do for a client who does not need additional income. The answer to this depends on the value of the Income Account relative to the account value. As demonstrated in the example in the previous chapter, if the Income Account is significantly higher than the account value – a term knows as "in the money" – then turning on the income might be the best investment recovery strategy. Put simply, driving the account value to zero as quickly as possible and then getting payments from the insurance company may easily provide the highest risk adjusted return on that particular asset.

If the account value and the Income Account are relatively close in value, then the best strategy is probably going to be to drop the living benefit rider completely (if the contract allows it). Why should your client pay for a living benefit rider if he or she knows he will not need the income that it guarantees? This is particularly true if the rider restricts the investment flexibility of the policyholder.

A client's full solvency throughout his or her retirement phase, without the need for annuities is not why you are reading this publication, so let's return to our deep dive on the things you need to know about living benefits.

5. Why Variable Annuity Companies Are So High on Volatility Managed Funds

An increasing number of variable annuity companies are requiring the use of volatility-managed sub-accounts if you choose a living benefit. The client brochures justify this by touting the benefits of the account value's steady growth. It will explain how the objective of these funds is to capture most of the upside of the market with less downside risk. Thus far, few of these funds, net of fees, have performed as promised. Given the high level of total fees along with an investment objective that puts more focus on protecting the downside than capturing the upside, many of the volatility funds are capturing most of the downside and only some of the upside. The insurance companies have all kinds of back testing to show that in the long run, these funds will work, but most of that data is based on a steady, thirty-year decline in interest rates. It seems likely that the next 30 years will be much different. While these volatility funds come in multiple flavors, they all rely heavily on a fixed income component of some kind as the primary means for smoothing returns. One of my colleagues likes to say, "These funds were built for yesterday's battle and will likely not perform as well in the battle yet to come."

While it's true that clients dislike volatility, variable annuity companies didn't add these sub-accounts because of client concerns. Over time, these volatility-managed funds may prove to be an attractive investment option, but the primary motivation to add these sub-accounts is to protect the insurance company from the next severe bear market. Essentially, these sub-accounts shift much of the risk that was borne by the insurance company in previous product designs to the policyholder. In fact, I believe that by requiring policyholders to invest in volatility managed funds when a living benefit is added to the policy, the insurance company is asking the policyholder to absorb much of its own hedging costs in addition to paying a specific fee for the rider itself.

And speaking of hedging, it is time to discuss why it is essential to add an aggressive investment strategy to a living benefit rider on a variable annuity.

6. Got a Variable Annuity with a Living Benefit? Invest Aggressively

Annuities are all about mitigating risk, which is especially true when the contract is a variable annuity. A living benefit on a variable annuity is designed to protect against a severe bear market like we experienced in both 2000-2002 and 2007-2009. It's when the account value falls the most that the living benefit becomes the most valuable. Despite the drop in the account value, the lifetime income is still guaranteed. With the income protected against a market decline, the primary goal of the account value is to create an increase in the guaranteed income by growing faster than the growth rate of the Income Account. So, ask yourself, will you be more likely to accomplish that goal with a 60/40 allocation (or a volatility managed sub-account) or a 100% equity allocation? Clearly, the best long-term strategy is to invest as aggressively as possible.

In practice, "things" are not that simple, I know. First and foremost, this is a rationale investment philosophy, not an emotional one. Some of your clients might agree to the concept initially, but may feel very differently when their account value falls 30 percent. I will leave it to you to manage the behavioral finance part of the equation for each of your clients. It is also likely that you are going to have to sell this concept to your compliance department. Even if they agree with the concept, they are unlikely to allow you to put all of the client's variable annuity money into equities if that policy is linked to an account that has a "moderate" risk profile.

Obviously, I'm not suggesting that your clients should be 100 percent in equities. It is merely that if the client is willing to pay to "insure" the future income flow from the annuity, it makes sense from an asset allocation point of view to put the most aggressive part of that client's portfolio in the annuity. The less volatile part of the overall portfolio should reside outside of the annuity.

Don't expect smooth sailing for your client after you have decided to invest aggressively. It can be difficult to follow this strategy even if your compliance department will allow it. The insurance companies understand the potential risk. That's why they require you to use asset allocation models and/or volatility managed funds. But even if you choose a product that requires these investment restrictions, make sure you select the most aggressive option available.

Just one caveat about seeking growth: make sure that you and your client a strategy that passes the authenticity test.

7. When "Growth" Sub-accounts, Are Not Growth

As stated before, if you add a living benefit to a variable annuity, you are probably going to be required to select an asset allocation strategy. Odds are that these strategies will be assembled to suit different risk profiles. At least one will probably be labeled a "growth" strategy. Never assume that an asset allocation sub-account with the name "growth" in the title will indeed be a growth strategy recognized as such across the industry. It may well be "growth" relative only to the other allowed strategies. As an example, let's examine the prospectus of a variable annuity currently on the market. It describes one of its growth strategy sub-accounts as follows:

"The underlying funds invest primarily in equity securities and/or fixed income securities. Under normal circumstances, the Fund invests approximately 70% of its assets in underlying funds which invest primarily in equity securities (stocks) and approximately 30% of its assets in underlying funds which invest primarily in fixed income securities (bonds)."

In addition to the targeted 70/30 allocations, the fund has the ability to reduce the equity exposure during times of high volatility. The prospectus goes on to say, "*In situations of extreme market volatility, the exchange-traded futures could potentially reduce the Fund's net economic exposure to equity securities to 0%.*"

The bottom line is that just because a sub-account has the word "growth" in it; do not assume that it's going to perform like a true growth fund.

8. Death Benefit/Living Benefit Combinations Will Often Only Pay the Living *OR* the Death Benefit

Up until very recently, many variable annuity companies offered the ability to combine both a living and death benefit. For an extra fee, if the Income Account was higher than the regular death benefit, the beneficiary would receive the value of the Income Account paid out as the death benefit. On the surface, this appears to be a very attractive alternative. Not only can the policyholder receive lifetime income based on the Income Account, but also the beneficiary could receive the value of the Income Account upon death. As a simple example, if I put $100,000 into such a product and begin taking five percent annual income payments for life, I would know that my beneficiaries would get at least $100,000 when I die no matter what happens to my account value. This feature is far more valuable than the standard Return of Premium death benefit, because that benefit is reduced by any withdrawals. Not surprisingly, Death Benefit/Living Benefit combinations were often marketed as a perpetual bond with a death put.

But of course, there is a catch – and it's a very big one. The client literature typically states that the death benefit is paid provided there is still money in the account value when the policyholder dies. I've heard numerous wholesalers describe this condition by saying, "**you must have $1 in the account value when you die in order for the death benefit to be paid.**" Such a statement is accurate. And of course, the description in the client brochure is accurate as well. What often isn't said, however, is that many policyholders will have to choose between either continuing to receive the income under the living benefit or stopping the income and preserving the death benefit long before the account value approaches $1. It is a mandatory decision not often disclosed to policyholders.

A simple example demonstrates my point. Let's assume that Client A buys a $100,000 living-death benefit combo. The cost of the two riders is 1.75 percent. Let's further assume that Client A begins taking five percent withdrawals immediately. As a result of withdrawals, fees and market performance, by year 15, the account value is down to $20,000. How long will it take to fully liquidate the account value if the account value earns six percent on average? Let's do the math.

1. If the account value grows by six percent, then it will be $21,200 one year later

2. But Client A is withdrawing five percent of the Income Account, or $5,000

3. And, the 1.75 percent must be deducted as well. This fee is calculated on the 100,000 Income account and then subtracted from the account value. Therefore, we must also subtract $1,750

4. After all withdrawals and fees, the account value is reduced from $20,000 to $14,450

Extrapolating out to three more years, we would conclude that the account value would be reduced to zero. To preserve the death benefit, Client A must stop receiving the lifetime income prior to then.

But when does the client have to actually stop the income payments? Remember, the 1.75 percent fee for the riders will continue to be calculated based on the 100,000 Income Account and then deducted from the account value even after the income payments stop. Therefore, the choice has to be made long before Client A's account value gets to $1. In this example, depending upon Client A's life expectancy and the expected growth of the account value, the income payments may have to stop after the withdrawal reduced the account value to $14,450.

There is nothing wrong with using a living-death benefit combination, provided the policyholder understands the ramifications perfectly. A day will come where he or she may have to choose between continuing the lifetime income payments and preserving the death benefit for the beneficiary. If the policyholder does not understand this and is left financially stranded at a critical time, you may end up having a very uncomfortable conversation with that policyholder for failing to raise that red flag before he or she signed the contract.

Many advisors have told me that they utilize the living-death benefit combinations because they don't know at the time of purchase which one the client will need. If the client ends up needing additional income in retirement, they want to make sure the policy provides for a lifetime income that is guaranteed to grow. But if the client does not end up needing additional income, they want to provide a death benefit that is guaranteed to grow. Only by combining these two benefits can you cover these two contingencies. This was a much more attractive strategy prior to 2012 when the cost of the two riders was much lower. After the financial crises, variable annuity companies began to steadily increase the cost of these riders. By 2013, it was highly likely that a policyholder would be paying almost two percent for this strategy. Throw in 1.3 percent for the contract itself and about one percent in sub-account fees and you have a fee drag of possible more than four percent - even more if you factor in that the rider fee is assessed on the Income Account, which is typically higher than the account value. And finally, you have to remember that this fee drag will likely be on an investment allocation that is no more than 60-70 percent equities. Certainly, there are some situations where combining these riders together makes sense even at today's fee levels, however, I'm merely pointing out that it should not be standard operating procedure for every variable annuity an advisor sells.

One last point before I leave this topic. Make sure you know whether or not the variable annuity company you are using forces annuitization of the contract, and if so, at what age. Every contract states that if the client annuitizes the contract, the living and death benefits are cancelled. Therefore, even if the policyholder does not end up having to make a choice between continuing the income from the living benefit or preserving the death benefit, if she lives too long, the choice will be made for her.

9. The Dark Horse Issue: Insurance Companies Have the Discretion to Increase Fees

Fees, along with annuity products' often complex designs, top financial advisors' list of concerns about the products. Traditionally, insurance companies have had the ability to increase the annual fee of a living benefit only after the occurrence of a step up. Since a step up essentially resets the Income Account up to the new, higher account value, it only made sense that insurance companies could increase the costs at the time of the reset. Some companies, however, have now given themselves the ability to increase the living benefit fees basically anytime they want. Most of these designs give the policyholder the ability to refuse a fee increase and still maintain the current level of guaranteed income. The policyholder only gives up the right to any further income increases. However, a handful of companies have gone one step further. The terms of their living benefit state that the guaranteed income will be reduced if the policyholder does not accept the fee increase. Insurance companies accomplish this by reducing either the income payout rate or the income base itself. I would strongly suggest that you avoid these contracts. While a step up of guaranteed income is typically a good thing and will likely be something you recommend that the client accept, that will not always be the case under today's pricing. In some cases, the fee increase can be so steep, the client will actually end up paying more in annual fees than they will receive in additional income. When a policyholder chooses to decline a step up, he or she is already giving up an increase in guaranteed income. There is no reason to suffer a decline in guaranteed income as well.

Final Thoughts

After having laid out every conceivable caveat to adding a living benefit to annuities, I realize that I might be giving off the impression that I'm not in favor of the rider. That would be a very inaccurate conclusion! The reality is that I'm a big proponent of living benefits. Unless a retiree is extremely wealthy, he or she will need an income stream that is guaranteed for life. Annuity living benefits are a great way to accomplish this goal without giving up total control of the asset. In addition, living benefits on variable annuities can provide the peace of mind that can allow a client to remain fully invested even during the worst bear markets. For living benefits to perform as promised, however, they must be managed correctly. This task is complicated by the rules and restrictions that ultimately enable the insurance companies to offer these guarantees.

CHAPTER 12

WHAT ARE YOU WAITING FOR? TURN ON THE INCOME

No one really knows what percentage of annuities with living benefits have actually begun taking the income allowed under the rider. Based on what I've seen, I suspect the percentage could be as low as 25%. I'm usually told that the client has not started taking the income because either she doesn't need additional income or she will get even more guaranteed income by waiting. While both of those reasons can make perfect sense, for many clients, the best investment decision is to turn on the income anyway. Take the following actual case as an example:

Account Value: $57,295

Income Base: 121,972

Guaranteed Amount of Income: $6,098 (5% of the income base)

Age of Client: 73

If a 73-year old client walked into your office and asked if it was OK to withdraw 10.6% of his account value each and every year, what would you say? Unless you expected that he had a relatively short life expectancy, you would likely advise against this for fear that he would outlive his money. Given that, in the situation above, why would you do anything other than advise the client to start taking the income? As I stated in the chapter on living benefits, at the end of the day, a lifetime living benefit is nothing other than a systematic withdrawal percentage that is guaranteed for life. In the case above, the insurance company is guaranteeing that the policyholder can take $6,098, or 10.6% of the current value of the policy, each and every year for as long as he lives – even if the account value goes to $0. Given the life expectancy of a 73-year-old male (about 13 years), there's a good chance that the account value will indeed go to $0 before he dies. Yes, it's true that the client would get even more guaranteed income by waiting another year, but at some point, the client gets close enough to his actual date of death that he will not liquidate the account no matter what the withdrawal rate. In fact, that's exactly what the insurance company hopes happens.

The above case may seem like an extreme case, but I assure you it is not. Given the aggressive income growth rates insurance companies built into their products prior to 2009 along with the poor account value performance by all products during the financial crises and the mediocre performance by many products since the financial crises, it is not at all uncommon to see relatively young policyholders with account values significantly below the income base. For many of these clients, their best strategy to maximize the return on the annuity will be to turn on the income with the goal of driving the account value to $0 as quickly as possible, thereby requiring the insurance company to fund the remaining income payments from its general account.

The Best Income Strategy for Living Benefits in IRAs

For many clients, other than Social Security, their IRA is likely to be their biggest source of retirement income. The desire to insure that income against another significant drop in the market just prior to or during retirement is a very valid reason to purchase a variable annuity with a living benefit within an IRA. Surprisingly though, in many cases, when it becomes time to begin taking the income out of the IRA – either by choice or because the client is now forced to take required minimum distributions (RMDs), I often see the first withdrawals come from the IRA assets that are not invested in the annuity. Again, the reason given for this is typically because the client can get even more guaranteed income by waiting. However, I would suggest the best strategy will usually be to do the exact opposite. By taking as much of the RMD from the annuity as the rider will allow each year, the client will not only increase the likelihood that the annuity will be driven to $0, but will also be able to grow the uninsured assets in the IRA. The other assets will not have the investment restrictions that come with most variable annuities with living benefits, which over the long run, should lead to greater asset growth. This strategy allows the client to meet the current income needs from the insured income portion of the portfolio while growing the more liquid and more flexible assets for future income or estate needs.

CHAPTER 13
STRUCTURING AN ANNUITY CONTRACT

In the world of financial contracts, annuities designate a role to play for everyone. And sometimes one party will play dual roles, depending on the terms of the contract. A policy can have an owner, joint owner, contingent annuity, annuitant, joint annuitant, one or more beneficiaries and a contingent beneficiary. With all of these roles to play in an annuity, the methods of structuring the contracts abound. Despite the temptation to create extremely creative contract terms, my advice is always to keep it simple. In instances where I have seen a structure that leads to unanticipated consequences, it is because the advisor recommended something other than the most basic structure. Therefore, I recommend using only one of the following three structures. I should note that the choice could differ a bit depending upon whether the contract being purchased is an owner-driven contract or an annuitant-driven contract. An owner-oriented contract will trigger a death benefit upon the death of the owner, while an annuitant-driven contract will trigger a death benefit upon the death of the annuitant. You should always check with the insurance company about which party triggers the death benefit. As if things aren't confusing enough, changes in either the legal staff and/or operations systems, have caused some companies to have both owner-driven contracts and annuitant-driven contracts.

What the Tax Law Requires Upon the Death of the "Holder"

It appears that Congress, when passing laws that affect the distributions of annuities, has never understood that the owner of an annuity does not have to be the annuitant. There is nothing in the tax code that refers to these two designations. Instead it discusses the consequences and requirements when the "holder" dies. The industry has uniformly interpreted the "holder" to be the owner of the contract. Unfortunately, that is usually about the only part of contract structuring that the industry has adopted across the board. Some contracts are owner-driven, which means that the death benefit is triggered upon the death of the owner. Other contracts are annuitant-driven, thereby triggering a death benefit upon the death of the annuitant. The contract can be even more dynamic – or confusing – because if the contract is owner-driven, then the beneficiary of the owner could be the actual beneficiary or the annuitant, depending upon the terms that the insurance company puts into place.

The flexible dynamic of annuities can make the products confusing. To simplify and streamline the concept, let's summarize the inheritance transmission requirements under the tax code when the so-called holder dies. I explore these options in greater detail in the chapter on annuity taxation.

If the "beneficiary" is the spouse of the "holder"

Upon the death of the "holder" (owner), the beneficiary spouse can choose from among the following options:

1. Continue the contract as the new owner. Under this option, the spouse essentially steps into the shoes of the owner and would then name a new beneficiary.

2. Receive the death benefit. It's important to note that under this option the choice may or may not be a taxable event. You should always check with the insurance company as to the tax consequences of this choice.

3. Annuitize the contract within 12 months of the death of the holder

4. Arrange a five-year payout schedule for the death benefit. This option is similar to option #2, except that it allows the spouse to defer or spread out the taxes that would be due when the death benefit is paid. I will note that this option can be challenging for annuity companies to administer because they have to liquidate the annuity to process the death benefit, but they have to then find a way to keep it on their administration system. While helping your client weigh this option,

familiarize yourself with how the insurance company's administrative process and restrictions.

When the beneficiary is not a spouse

An annuity beneficiary can be anyone. A beneficiary with a different relationship to the so-called holder has all of the same options as the spouse except for the ability to continue the contract as the new owner. Essentially, the beneficiary must receive the death benefit either in a lump sum, over five years or in the form of annuity payments.

The non-qualified deferred stretch

Some companies have interpreted the tax code to mean that a non-spousal beneficiary can stretch the death benefit out over the life expectancy of the original owner. Because such an option isn't always allowed, and the rules can differ amongst the companies that do allow them, I'll merely list this as a possible option that is worth exploring with the issuing company. If the company does allow the contract to be stretched, make sure you ask the insurance company what their process is to make sure the money is taken out over the original owner's life expectancy.

Three Contract Structures that Will Keep You Out of Trouble

The beauty of the following three methods is that the result should be the same whether it's an owner-driven contract or an annuitant-driven contract.

Therefore, they should not create the possibility of an unforeseen consequence upon the death of the "holder". However, since it's not possible to know how every annuity company interprets their own contracts, it's always a good idea to verify the outcomes of any contract structure you use.

1. Single owner with a spouse as the beneficiary

Owner: Client

Annuitant: Client

Beneficiary: Client's Spouse

Contingent Beneficiary: Whomever the client wants to have the money if the client and spouse die together

In this scenario the client is both the owner and annuitant, so when the client dies, the money will pass to the spouse as the beneficiary. As a spousal beneficiary, the spouse can choose between taking over the ownership of the contract and taking the death benefit. If the spouse takes over the contract as the new owner and annuitant, then the spouse would then name his or her beneficiary. The contingent beneficiary comes into play only if both spouses die together. Under such a situation, without a contingent beneficiary, the contract would go to the estate of the beneficiary and therefore will not bypass probate.

2. Joint ownership between spouses

Joint Owners: Both spouses
Annuitant: Spouse #1
Joint Beneficiaries: Both spouses
Contingent Beneficiary: Whomever the joint owners want to inherit the money if they both die together

This structure works in the same manner as the first example. By naming both spouses' joint beneficiaries, they both have the option of continuing the contract when the other spouse dies. If the contract is an annuitant-driven contract, then there are some advantages to naming the spouse with the shortest life expectancy as the annuitant. This will trigger the death benefit upon the most likely first death. If it's a variable annuity and the guaranteed death benefit exceeds the account value, then the death benefit would be payable to the surviving spouse. Such an event is even more likely if the contract has an enhanced death benefit rider. Even on a contract with no guaranteed death benefit such as a fixed or indexed annuity, there can be some advantages to having the money available to the beneficiary without a surrender charge. If it's an owner-driven contract, then the selected annuitant does not matter. The surviving spouse as the joint owner will have the option of receiving the death benefit or continuing the contract.

3. Single owner with a non-spouse beneficiary

Owner: Client

Annuitant: Client

Beneficiary: Son or daughter, next of kin, or whoever gets the money when the owner/annuitant dies

Since the owner and annuitant is one in the same, this structure will work identically no matter if the contract is owner-driven or annuitant-driven. As a non-spousal beneficiary, the son/daughter can receive the death benefit within a year, annuitize the contract or continue it for up to five years in order to spread the taxes out.

You will note that in every one of the above examples, the owner and the annuitant are the same person. If you find yourself considering any structure other one of the structures listed above, my advice is simple – don't. But if you insist, make sure you first reach out to the insurance company and examine all of the possible outcomes of the structure you are considering.

The Dangerous of Having An Annuitant That Is Different Than An Owner

Virtually every problematic structure I have ever seen occurs when the owner and annuitant are different people. This is typically done either because the advisor is trying to purchase a contract for someone that would otherwise be too old to be the annuitant or because the advisor is attempting to extend the tax deferral through another generation. Unfortunately, both of these goals are difficult to accomplish, if not impossible, given today's tax laws and contract structures. To begin with, insurance companies don't want to issue contracts to older individuals because from an actuarial standpoint, it is unlikely that the contract will remain in force long enough for the company to recoup the commission that was fronted when the policy was issued. Therefore, the only way a company will issue the contract to a 90-year-old is if the death benefit payout is contingent by the death of the annuitant rather than the owner. When the 90-year-old owner dies, the contract will continue, albeit with a new owner. Also, under the current tax code, only a spouse beneficiary can continue a contract for more than five years after the death of the "holder". Even if you list the owner's child as the annuitant, therefore, when the 90-year-old "holder" dies, unless there is a joint owner, it is likely that the insurance company will require you to receive the proceeds within five years of the death of the 90-year-old.

If a contract has different people as owner and annuitant, how the proceeds are distributed will depend upon who dies first – the owner or the annuitant - and who the insurance company considers to be the beneficiary of the deceased. On an annuitant-driven contract, the beneficiary is almost always the actual beneficiary listed on the contract. However, on an owner-driven contract, the beneficiary could be the joint owner, the annuitant or a listed beneficiary. The tax code merely requires a distribution to the beneficiary upon the death of the "holder". Who the beneficiary of the "holder" is under the contract depends on how the insurance company decides to define it within the contract itself. Not knowing in advance how the contract will be interpreted can lead to very bad consequences.

Following is the most common example of a contract structure gone wrong.

Annuitant different than the owner:

Owner: Client

Annuitant: Spouse

Beneficiary: Child

This structure is often selected if the client is too old to be the annuitant, but the younger spouse (or other young individual) is still young enough to be the annuitant. If this structure was used because the owner was too old to be the annuitant, then it's likely to be an annuitant-driven contract. If it does happen to be an owner-driven contract, then it is unlikely that a death benefit will be paid (and therefore no surrender charge is waived) upon the death of the owner. In addition, the proceeds will go to the party that the contract designates as the beneficiary of the owner. If the beneficiary of the owner is the annuitant and the goal is to have the proceeds of the annuity go to the spouse upon death, then this structure might work. I say "might" because while the spouse would end up owning the contract, the guaranteed death benefit would be due only if the death benefit is triggered by the death of the owner, which is unlikely. If it is triggered by the death of the annuitant, then the spouse would be taking over the contract based on the current value rather than the potentially higher death benefit.

This contract structure can present potentially serious consequences under two other possible circumstances. First, the contract is owner-driven and the beneficiary is considered to be the beneficiary of the owner, then the money will bypass the spouse and go to the child as the beneficiary. Second, if this is an annuitant-driven contract, and the annuitant (spouse) dies before the owner, the money will most certainly pass to the child. Not only will the owner lose control of the money, but since he or she is still alive, he or she has also made a taxable gift to the beneficiary. Talk about estate planning gone bad.

But what if the spouse is also too old to be the annuitant, and therefore the child is listed as the annuitant instead? Such a structure might look as follows:

Owner: Client
Annuitant: Child
Beneficiary: Spouse

Will this work? Once again, it will depend upon whom the insurance company designates as the beneficiary of the owner. If the annuitant is the beneficiary of the owner, then upon the death of the owner, control of the policy will pass to the child and bypass the spouse. If the **spouse** is deemed to be the beneficiary of the owner, then the spouse will gain control of the contract and everything should be fine (although, it is possible that no death benefit will be paid). If this is an annuitant-driven contract (which is likely), then if the child dies first, then the proceeds pass to the spouse. That's probably OK too, but you had better make sure that your client and his or her spouse get along!

If You Insist On Having Different Owners and Annuitants

If for some reason you have determined it is necessary to separate the roles of the owner and the annuitant, then I must stress the need to contact the insurance company before the policy is issued. Also, have the insurance company send you hypothetical case studies that explain all of the possible scenarios of the contract as structured. No matter how the insurance company interprets the contract, the following structure will give you the maximum protection against an unanticipated and potentially detrimental outcome.

Owner: Client
Joint Owner: Spouse
Annuitant: Child
Joint Beneficiaries: Client and Spouse
Contingent Beneficiary: Child

Should either the client or spouse die first, then the remaining joint owner will take over the contract as the sole owner and the contract will continue in force. Unless the insurance company has a generous administrative policy, in all likelihood, since a joint owner and the annuitant are still alive, the insurance company is unlikely to pay out a death benefit. Should the child unexpectedly die first, then the proceeds are paid to the client and spouse as the beneficiaries. Again, whether a death benefit is payable will depend upon whether this is an owner or annuitant-driven contract. Unless some insurance company has a unique interpretation (which is always possible), this structure should guarantee that proceeds are not paid to the wrong person upon the first or even second death.

What If An Existing Contract Has the Wrong Structure?

If you find one of your clients has a contract structure that you suspect will lead to an undesired outcome, then your first step should be to call the insurance company and explore your options for changing the arrangement. Changing owners on a contract is usually easy to do administratively. If it causes the control of the policy to change from one person to another, however, it is likely to create a taxable event. Many companies will allow you to change the annuitant only if it is an owner-driven contract. And even then, they might insist that the annuitant remain the same. If that's the case, it might be possible to fix the structure by changing the beneficiary to maximize the likelihood that the right person will ultimately get the proceeds. One thing is for sure, very little can be done once the first death occurs. While the insurance company will likely agree that the structure does not comply with the owner's intent, without a court order, they will be unable to change the terms of the contract.

Did You Find This Chapter Confusing?

Annuity structures are not always straightforward. Arranging and administering them can put even the best advisors to the test. The vague tax code that only recognizes the "holder" of an annuity, combined with the multiple possible structures and the lack of standardization between companies as to how the administer death claims can inadvertently create a minefield for advisors selling annuities. Do yourself and your clients a favor – keep the structure simple. Never try to circumvent a tax law or an insurance company's rules by getting creative with an annuity structure. The potential pitfalls are not worth the risk.

CHAPTER 14

COMMON ANNUITY OBJECTIONS – FACT OR FICTION?

Few financial products match annuities for their ability to polarize opinions of the "experts". At one end of the spectrum we have individuals like Ken Fisher of Fisher Investments (who is currently taking out full page newspaper ads touting "I HATE annuities, and you should too") and Suze Orman who has frequently expressed her disdain for annuities over the years. On the other end of the spectrum are the thousands of insurance agents who insist that no retirement plan should be without an annuity of some kind. Such extreme positions always lead to distortions of the truth. To ascertain the truth, let's look at the validity of the most common criticisms of annuities. I will first note that many of the harshest critics of annuities have a bad habit of confusing the attributes of variable, indexed and immediate annuities. This is usually due to ignorance about how the products work or a desire to generalize in order to make their point (or both). Therefore, I will strive to make it clear when an objection applies only to a specific product line.

1. Annuities are illiquid

When assessing common objections to annuities, it seems appropriate to start with what is probably the most common misconception about annuities – they are illiquid. This objection is most certainly one of the concern's FINRA has about annuities. In FINRA's view, the tax liability that comes with any withdrawal is a cost, hence every annuity is illiquid. As a result, FINRA insists that all broker/dealers assess the amount of "liquid" assets a client has in order to determine if the "illiquid" annuity recommendation is in the client's best interest. Certainly, there are types of annuities that are illiquid. Immediate annuities and deferred income annuities work partly because their illiquidity allows insurance companies to better forecast the liability and therefore better price the product for the policyholder. If an individual has even a potential need for liquidity, then immediate and deferred income annuities would not be an appropriate income solution. To label all annuities as illiquid is just silly. Let's discuss why, beginning with the fact that virtually every deferred annuity (other than DIAs) allows for a 10% annual withdrawal without incurring any early withdrawal penalty (surrender charge). Also, if a policyholder finds that the withdrawal amount cannot meet his or her immediate cash needs, it is always possible to elect to pay the surrender charge and cash in the policy. Any reasonable priced annuity would therefore allow the policyholder to receive at least 90-95% of the account value. That hardly sounds illiquid to me. Most annuities have a surrender charge period of 7-10 years. Many are less than that. Once an annuity gets beyond the surrender charge period, the policyholder can get the full account value at any time within days of requesting the funds. True enough, a policyholder is not likely to be happy about paying any surrender charges, but annuities are hardly alone as a financial product that has a penalty or cost to cash in prior to maturity. Indeed, due to the possible surrender charges and deferred taxes, an annuity should be tapped for funds only as a last resort, but if the client does have an urgent need for funds, most annuities can provide virtually all of its value.

2. Annuities should never be placed in a qualified plan

Aside from the perceived obstacles to gaining access to funds in the annuity, skeptics also raise objections to their inclusion in tax deferred qualified plans. On the surface, this objection makes perfect sense. Since every asset within a qualified plan gains the tax deferral that comes with the plan, the annuity loses one of its greatest benefits. In the absolute sense this is true – but it would be hasty to assert that annuities should never be placed in a qualified plan, because such an assertion assumes that the annuity offers no other benefits other than tax deferral. Whether or not an investment should be placed into a retirement plan depends on the client's specific retirement goals, not the tax characteristics of the investment itself. As an example, no one would ever suggest that individual stocks are inappropriate options for an IRA despite the fact that you are turning potential long-term capital gains into ordinary income, because individual stocks meet the goal of providing growth potential. An annuity needs to be looked at in the same manner. The appropriate question is when would an annuity make sense in a qualified plan?

a. Variable Annuities – While variable annuities offer a multitude of investment options and fund managers, it's usually possible to get equivalent investment options outside of a variable annuity at a cheaper cost. Therefore, the investment options alone are usually not a sufficient reason. There are some exceptions, however. For example, some variable annuities offer investment options that are not available to retail clients. Other variable annuities may offer a unique asset allocation model. However, generally speaking, the value of variable annuities are often derived from other features that cannot be easily replicated by other investment solutions. Historically, the guaranteed death benefits have justified the investment. Cheaper and simpler investment options are available to investors, but only a variable annuity guarantees a return of investment (or more) upon death. Since 2002, it's been the living benefits that have justified the use within a qualified plan. Every IRA (except Roth IRAs) are subject to minimum required withdrawals. If you are required to take an annual income whether you want to or not, why not insure that income by adding a living benefit?

b. <u>Fixed and Indexed Annuities</u> – Whether a fixed and/or indexed annuity belongs in a retirement plan depends entirely upon the expected return of the annuity given the risk characteristics of these products. Similarly, if CDs or bonds are appropriate investment options for inclusion in retirement plans, a fixed and indexed annuity can also be equally appropriate. Fixed and indexed annuities will typically earn 2%-3% more than a CD and they don't carry the interest risk that comes with traditional fixed income investments.

c. <u>Immediate and Deferred Income Annuities</u> –The appropriateness of these options depends entirely upon how the client wants to take the income out of the annuity. While the RMD calculations ensure that a check of some amount will be received for the client's lifetime, the client might appreciate the certainty that comes with these annuity products. And now that Treasury has established new rules for Qualified Longevity Annuity Contracts (see the immediate annuity chapter for details on QLACs), deferred income annuities can provide additional flexibility for those that want to minimize their RMD amounts.

Those that subscribe to objection #1 will often say that the illiquid nature of the annuity will make it an unsuitable option for retirement plans despite other very practical and attractive features. My question to those skeptics is: "Why is the liquidity necessary in the first place?" If the goal is to keep every asset within the plan as liquid as possible so that you can reallocate money within the plan at will, then I would agree with this statement (although I would question the strategy). If, however, the goal of the liquidity is to enable the client to tap money from his or her qualified plan in an emergency, then I would argue every asset in the plan is equally illiquid. Any potential taxes and penalties are a function of the retirement plan itself, not the nature of the investment within the plan. Therefore, if the client's needs are so great that taxes are not a concern, it's unlikely that a surrender charge will be a concern either.

3. Annuities are expensive

"Annuities can carry fees of 3%-4% per year", say the detractors. When you hear this objection, the critic is typically referring to variable annuities. Since all of the fees on other types of annuities are built into the spread, the equivalent objection on these products is that the rates of return are too low. With fixed and indexed annuities, unless you add a living benefit, the quoted rates or caps are net of all fees, therefore the rates are the rates. It's easy, therefore to determine if they are too low. Hence, I'll focus this section on variable annuities.

Variable annuities are far from cheap. The annual fees on the core product and the underlying sub-accounts will range from 2%-3% depending on the annuity share class and the type of sub-account. Throw in any living and/or enhanced death benefits and total fees can be 3%-4.5% per year. However, it's important to realize that the client is getting more than just a mutual fund alternative when riders are added to the policy. You are now layering in insurance that is not available on any other investment. Whether or not the investment options plus the extra benefits are worth 3%-4.5% per year is a source of endless debate. I'll leave it for you to decide based on your client's needs. Here are the questions that you, as the financial advisor need to ask:

- If the investor is purchasing the annuity without additional benefits, are the investment options, tax deferral, tax-free transfers between the investment options and the return of premium death benefit worth 0.5%-1.5% more per year than a mutual fund?

- If the investor is buying the additional benefits, are the benefits plus the guarantee of systematic withdrawals for life and/or an enhanced death benefit worth 1.5%-2.5% more per year than other investments (i.e., mutual funds)?

4. Annuities pay large commissions

The inference here is that the large commissions equates to bad consumer value. Since the commission is built into the annuity's cost structure, the investor pays for the commission in the form of lower returns, just as he or she would with any other commissionable product. The real question therefore is, are annuity commissions too large to justify their benefits? Most annuities offer a commission option that allows the agent to receive all of the commission upfront. These upfront commissions can be as high as 7% on variable annuities and 10-12% on some indexed annuities (although most index annuity commissions are now more in line with variable annuity commissions). Anytime you see an upfront commission of 7% or more, the first reaction is going to be "wow, that's a lot" – particularly in today's increasingly no-load or direct purchase world. The insurance companies have inadvertently added fuel to this argument by bucking the trend within the financial services industry of ever tightening commissions. When variable annuities were first made readily available in the early 1980's, the standard commission was 4% without a trail, thereby making variable annuities the only investment that has seen an increase in commission over time.

However, before you conclude that annuities pay a large commission, it's important that you understand the pricing behind the product. The average annuity will remain in force for 2-3 years passed the surrender charge period. Therefore, a variable annuity with a 7-year surrender charge and a 7% commission, is likely to stay on the insurance company's books for 10 years. This would mean the selling agent should expect to receive the equivalent of 0.70% per year in commission. In a world where a 1% fee on assets is the norm, perhaps the policyholder isn't getting such a bad deal. In addition, most annuities offer multiple commission options. In addition, to an option that pays all of the commission upfront, that same annuity might allow the advisor to choose something like 5% upfront with a 0.25% trail or 4% with a 0.50% trail. These options seem more reasonable and therefore don't get as much criticism. However, from a cost point of view, they are all equivalent.

5. Annuities are complex

Annuities continually land on FINRA's list of complex products, so it follows that they are complex, right? The reality is that annuities can be as simple or complex as you want them. A basic annuity with no extra bells and whistles is really quite simple. For example, advisory annuities pay no commissions, has no surrender charges, and typically charge only a small fee to cover administration. How "complex" is that? Now, I grant you that if you load up a variable annuity with multiple living and death benefit options and various fee schedules based on those options, the contract can get very complex very fast. This is also true with index annuities that offer multiple index options and 3-5 different interest crediting strategies. I would argue however, that the added complexity is the cost of being offered options and flexibility. Think about the last time you bought tooth paste or even Oreo cookies (if you haven't bought Oreos recently, I suggest you wander down the cookie aisle at your grocery store next time you are there – you will be amazed at the variety of Oreos that now exist). The choices seem endless. But would we better off if we returned to the world of one kind of Crest toothpaste in a single flavor? I know we wouldn't be better off with just the original Oreo, because in my opinion the person that thought of Double Stuff Oreos belongs in the cookie hall of fame (and the mint things are pretty darn good too).

My point is that complex should not be equated with detrimental. It just means that you have to take the time to understand the various options and learn when they do and don't make sense.

6(a). Annuities are a hidden tax time bomb and 6(b) Variable annuities turn capital gains into ordinary income and cost the policyholder the opportunity to get a stepped up cost basis at death

These objections are covered in detail in the chapter on tax deferral. To summarize here in order to make this chapter complete, I would suggest the following:

- Annuities give the policyholder the flexibility to choose when to pay the taxes

- Given the complexity of filing taxes, clients always appreciate the ability to forgo a 1099 each year. In addition, if you think of all of the looming federal costs of supporting the baby boomers continue to move into retirement, I could make a case for the need to reduce your clients' financial footprint. Tax deferral is a good way to do that.

- The annual 1099s issued by mutual funds each year are just as likely to generate short term capital gains as long terms gains – especially if the fund has a high turnover rate. And how much fun is it to explain to clients why they have to pay taxes on a mutual fund that has actually fallen in value?

- Deferred earnings within an annuity do not impact taxes on social security, the 3.8% investment income created by the Affordable Care Act and potential taxes on social security income.

- Medicare premiums are determined by the client's annual reportable income. High income individuals can pay up to 4 times as much in monthly Medicare premiums than those with low levels of reportable income. Annuity assets are not included in the income calculation until they are withdrawn from the annuity and become taxable.

Summary

Like any other investment, annuities have inherent limitations. Insurance companies are very creative when it comes to product design. This creativity leads to both unique benefits and complexity. As long as the pricing structure requires the insurance company to front the commission out of its own pocket, some will perceive the surrender charges as too high and too long – especially if that same critic perceives the commission as too high. And since annuities are sold rather than bought, the insurance companies must build an extensive and expensive sales, marketing and support structure – all of which comes at a cost to the policyholder. Despite all of this, until Congress seriously undertakes real tax reform and as long as people have a need for a guaranteed income for life, avoid interest rate risk and are not satisfied with what they can earn at the bank, then annuities will be in demand.

CHAPTER 15
IMPORTANT THINGS THAT ARE OFTEN LEFT UNSAID

If you want to sell something – in this or any other product-driven industry – one rule of thumb is to point up the benefits of your product and divert attention away from the product's potential negatives. Not surprisingly, therefore, there are aspects of annuities that insurance companies and their representatives do not take great pains to tell you. Unfortunately, these omissions can cause you and your clients headaches down the road. I've touched on a few of these situations in previous chapters, but it makes sense to consolidate them all in one chapter as an easy reference guide. So, let's dive into the things that are most likely to keep an annuity from performing as planned.

1. More annuity policies will be annuitized than you think

Annuity contracts have always required an annuitization age – typically 85, 90 or 95 years old. Up until this century, virtually every insurance company had an administrative practice of waiving this age. This approach made complete sense for all parties involved, because the insurance companies want to hold onto the money as long as possible. Why force a policyholder to liquidate an account in the form of annuity payments if that policyholder doesn't want or need the income? But the financial equation changed after the Dotcom Crash of 2000. Suddenly, many of these insurance companies found themselves with policies with death benefits significantly higher than the account value. It was even worse for the companies whose policies that had death benefits that were reduced dollar-for-dollar by any withdrawals. At the suggestion of the variable annuity wholesalers—who are always quick to pass on a new strategy—advisors had their clients strip most of the account value out of these policies. This tactic creates situations where account values as little as $5,000 support death benefits of $100,000 — or more. Naturally, the pricing actuaries became worried about such an imbalance. They realized that the contract listed a maximum annuitization date. Waiving that date was a company practice, not a contractual guarantee. Suddenly, most companies ceased waiving the maximum annuitization date. When an annuity contract is annuitized, the policyholder essentially exchanges the account value for the specified annuity payments. When the account value disappears, so does the death benefit. All of a sudden, despite years of assurances by the company wholesalers that this would never occur, many insurance companies found it expedient to no longer waive the maximum annuitization date.

Insurance companies justified this change by stating that the Internal Revenue Service, or IRS, had threatened to tax the inside buildup of any contract that did not require annuitization at a specific age. As for why the IRS would do that, the logic behind this was quite simple: the tax code affords tax deferral to annuities as an incentive to save for retirement, therefore if the contract doesn't require annuity payments at some point, it is really not acting as an annuity and therefore should not be tax deferred. In my opinion, there is only one problem with this logic: As best as I can tell, the IRS simply does not care about this issue. During my first 20 years in this business – all of which were spent working with various annuity companies – I continually heard about the IRS' concern with this issue from insurance company lawyers and actuaries. The only party I've never heard it from is the IRS. In fact, I've even had direct conversations with Treasury on this issue, and each time they have assured me that this issue is nowhere near their radar. Unfortunately, they have never been willing to put this in writing. And without something definitive on this issue from Treasury, the insurance companies will continue to take the most conservative position possible on this issue – particularly since such a position benefits them. Now the insurance companies have a new excuse for requiring annuitization: Some now claim that the agreements they have reached with the states regarding the need to escheat property requires them to force annuitization per the terms of the contract. Given that there is no need to escheat an asset for which the insurance company knows that the policyholder is alive, I have yet to figure out how this would or should affect annuitization, but it has become the policy of many insurers nonetheless.

This sets up a tough situation for policyholders; especially those who are approaching the annuitization date and don't need or want the money? What can you do if that situation applies to your client? Unfortunately, not much. The only option is to surrender the contract or execute a 1035 exchange before the annuitization date. Surrendering the contract will cause all of the deferred taxes due, so that is rarely a good option. That leaves only a 1035 exchange as a possible solution. Just be aware that, it is not easy to find a company that will issue a contract on anybody that old and not require annuitization itself. I am aware of just one company that will issue fixed annuities up to age 100 and not require annuitization, so it is worth the time to check your product platform.

2. Required Minimum Distributions Can Kill Living and Death Benefits

Equally important to knowing when to activate the income on a living benefit is calculating the RMD amount. In 2004, the Treasury Department issued new rules for calculating required minimum distributions for annuity contracts. Essentially, this new provision requires the insurance company to calculate the RMD based on the account value plus the present value of the living benefit or death benefit – or both, depending on the policy – if the present value of those benefits exceeds the account value by at least 20 percent (**Reg. 1.401(a)(9)-6**). Good luck getting any insurance company to explain to you its method of applying this calculation! The empirical assumptions that could be used for this calculation vary widely among insurance companies, and each firm guards its own assumptions as vigilantly as if they had discovered the fountain of youth! For your purposes, and for those of your clients, all you need to know is that if the Income Account on a death benefit or living benefit is greater than the account value, the RMD will be based on an amount greater than the account value. Therefore, your client will have to take out more from the annuity each year than he or she would otherwise. In extreme cases, this higher RMD can cause the owner to liquidate the account value well before his life expectancy. And remember, once the account value is liquidated, any additional death benefit is eliminated as well.

Let's explore an example:

Client A is 75 years old and has a variable annuity with a guaranteed death benefit of $150,000, but an account value of just $100,000.

Without the death benefit, Client A would have to withdraw 4.4% of the account value, or $4,400. The higher death benefit, however, requires that he take out significantly more – perhaps as much as 30 percent more. It's not hard to see how these higher withdrawals will likely cause the annuity to be fully liquidated well before the client reaches his life expectancy. Ironically, if this occurs, no death benefit will be paid and by that time it will be clear that all of the RMD amounts were based on values that had no relationship in reality.

Sadly, also, unless the client can take these RMD amounts from other IRA assets, short of ignoring the calculated RMD amount, losing the death benefit is inevitable.

You might be wondering why the U.S. Department of the Treasury changed industry guidelines for calculating RMDs. By definition, an RMD is a % of the value of the IRA. There is clearly an economic value to both the living and death benefit, therefore it does make sense to include an additional amount in the calculation. In addition, the IRS used the same definition to value annuities for Roth IRA conversions. On the surface, it makes sense to value an annuity for RMD purposes in the same manner as they are valued for Roth conversions. Where the Treasury errored is that they gave the insurance companies too much latitude on how this value is calculated. Had Treasury been more prescriptive, this problem would not exist. The RMD calculation is supposed to be done as a percentage of the client's life expectancy. It's designed so that it cannot liquidate the IRA prior to the death of the client. However, the insurance companies do not take into consideration the likelihood that death benefit won't be paid because of the calculation itself. Therefore, they are overvaluing the economic value of the living and death benefit. Take the real-life example of the 83-year-old with an account value of $2,452 and a death benefit of $40,705. The insurance company valued the RMD at $920, almost six times the value of the RMD without the death benefit. With such an RMD, the policy will clearly lapse in no more than three years. Given that, what is the likelihood that the death benefit will actually be paid? An 83-year-old has a life expectancy of about 7 years. Therefore, there is less than a 50% possibility that the death benefit will be paid prior to the account value going to $0. However, the insurance company's calculation sees to assume that there is a 100% probability it will be paid.

Had the Treasury Department understood all of this in 2004, I am confident that the entity would have reached a different conclusion. After all, if the death benefit goes away, the tax liability does as well. The only party that wins here is the insurance company, because it will be far less likely to have to pay out the death benefit. The policyholder will likely lose the death benefit and the U.S. Treasury will lose out on the taxes that would have been paid on that benefit.

3. Volatility Managed Sub-Accounts Greatly Reduce the Odds of Getting A Step Up

After weathering the financial Crisis of 2007-2008, the Great Recession that followed into 2009, and today's persistently low interest rates, the financial industry readjusted its response to risk and volatility. Many variable annuity companies, in particular, have required volatility-managed sub-accounts as a means to reduce the attendant risks of providing living benefits. By placing a volatility overlay on an asset allocation model, the insurance company can eliminate wide swings in the account value. While this approach can come in many different flavors, essentially what they do is reallocate money from equities to fixed income when market volatility increases and reallocate money back to equities when market volatility falls. This means that at any given time a sub-account can be as much as 90 percent equities or as little as 10 percent. In all likelihood, it will average out to a 40 percent-50 percent equity allocation.

The insurance companies will say that this investment approach is appealing because most clients prefer steady returns rather than large swings in the account value. While this is certainly true, it also means the policyholder is essentially buying insurance on insurance. By paying to add a living benefit to a variable annuity, the policyholder is already paying for insurance on his or her future income stream. Muting the potential earnings by adding a volatility overlay to an asset allocation model only further insures that future income. Essentially, the insurance company is requiring the policyholder to cover the cost that it incurs to hedge the living benefit by requiring him or her to both pay the living benefit fee and give up much of the potential upside of any account value growth. If the policyholder's income is already protected from a significant drop in the account value, why also relinquish the upside potential that can lead to more income as a result of a step up?

Essentially, if you take a 60/40 portfolio, add a volatility overlay and then charge a rider fee of 1 percent-1.5 percent annually, it becomes very difficult for the account value to increase faster than the guaranteed growth of the Income Account. This design essentially turns a variable annuity with a living benefit into an index annuity with a living benefit. If that were the end result, the client would typically be better off by simply buying the index annuity in order to get the higher guaranteed income from the start.

CHAPTER 16

WHAT HAPPENS IF AN ANNUITY COMPANY GOES OUT OF BUSINESS?

Bankruptcies are complicated procedures for any business sector, and potentially byzantine when that company specializes in annuities. **The solution to a complicated question begins with a very basic answer.** All annuities issued by insurance companies that are members of the guarantee association of the policyholder's individual state guarantee fund are covered under that fund. The policy owner's state of residence – not the jurisdiction in which the contract was purchased – dictates which rules apply. The amount of coverage varies from state to state, but "withdrawal and cash values of annuities are covered up to at least $100,000 per person per company" according to the National Organization of Life & Health Insurance Guaranty Association. It is not uncommon, however, for some states to cover up to $500,000, and you can find a complete list of the individual coverage by state at http://www.nolhga.com/. The guarantee is similar to the FDIC's coverage of bank deposits.

State insurance regulations prohibit talking about the guarantee association at the time of sale. If a client asks about the guarantee association, advisors are allowed to refer him or her to the NOLHGA website, but the guidance ends there. As it's been explained to me, financially sound insurance companies are concerned that a lightly capitalized company will attempt to recklessly sell policies based on the guarantee, thereby creating a liability for the industry should the company go under. Admittedly that logic is hard to follow. After all, the ability to extoll the virtues of FDIC insurance has never in itself led to a wave of bank failures.

Either the guarantee exists or it does not. Obviously, it does, so why not give policyholders the peace of mind that comes with that knowledge?

How does the state rehabilitation process work?

No process is ever the same, so there is no single definitive answer to this question. If you inquire with any individual state guarantee fund, it will refer you to a bunch of vaguely written statutes. However, we can look at previous situations as a guide for what is likely to happen. (Fortunately, few examples of annuity company bankruptcy proceedings exist. However, this also means that without much precedence there is also little guidance on a likely process.) Believe it or not, one example involves Baldwin United, the piano company. Back in the early 1980's, Baldwin owned two insurance companies that sold mostly fixed annuities. Unfortunately, their portfolio that was heavily weighted with junk bonds could not ultimately pay the interest rates guaranteed by the policies. In 1983, the insurance companies were placed into "rehabilitation" by the states of Arkansas and Indiana. These states got to experience the joy of managing the process because they happened to be the states in which the companies were domiciled. The domiciled state always has the responsibility of coordinating the efforts of all of the states in which the policyholders reside. The objective of the process is to make the policyholders whole as quickly as possible. If a sound company is willing and able to take over the troubled company, the states will arrange for that to occur. If the problem is too big and therefore no company is willing to step in, then the states take over the company with the goal of nursing the company back to financial health. That can take months or years. In the case of the Baldwin United companies it took years.

At this point it should be mentioned that the state guarantee associations have very little in cash reserves available to fix any new problem companies. As money is needed, each state assesses the member companies a fee based on the premiums written in that particular state. However, there is a maximum that each company can be assessed in any one year. Therefore, if the problem is too big it can take several years of assessments before policyholders can be made whole. That is in fact what happened with the Baldwin companies. Eventually, the regulators improved the financials of the companies to the point where New York-based MetLife became willing to take over the policies.

Much can be learned by the steps that state regulators took in the Baldwin case. The first step was to suspend all policyholder liquidations with three notable exceptions. They allowed 1) annuitization payments to continue, 2) death benefits to be paid and 3) liquidations based on financial needs. All other policyholders found their funds frozen. After that the regulators reduced the amount of interest credited to the policyholders. Admittedly, these policies had certain rate guarantees, but in a rehabilitation process, the states have the right to change these guarantees. Finally, they hired Goldman Sachs to restructure the portfolio by selling off many of the higher yielding junk bonds and replacing them with shorter maturity government and corporate bonds. In retrospect, given that steadily falling interest rates over the next 30 years created perhaps the greatest bull market for bonds ever, this decision by Goldman was a mistake, but it certainly made sense at the time. Over time, these actions reduced the gap between the assets and liabilities of the company. Eventually, that gap was small enough that MetLife was willing to take over the policies, at which point the money once again became available for each policyholder. Each policyholder was given the option of swapping their annuity for a new MetLife annuity or simply cashing out.

Note: While policyholders had their funds frozen for a number of years and their interest rates reduced, they did continue to earn interest during the process and no one received less money than they had put into the annuity. In fact, everyone received more than the value they had at the time of the rehabilitation.

This process tells us three important things:

1. No policyholder is likely to lose money in the strict sense of the word, but a policyholder that earns less interest than expected and can't access his or her funds, might have a different perspective.

2. Contract terms can be changed if the regulators deem it a necessary step.

3. The entire process can be tedious and complex and can take years to resolve.

What about variable annuities?

Variable annuities, which represent a significant segment of the market, must be addressed. No company with a sizeable variable annuity block has ever gone into rehabilitation. Therefore, opinions vary on what would actually happen. Prior to the invention of living benefits, the "what if a company goes under" question as it pertains to variable annuities was simply not a big deal. Since the variable annuity assets reside in the insurance company's separate account, the rehabilitation process should have little, if any impact on variable annuity policyholders. The purpose of the separate account is to make sure the variable annuity assets are available only to the variable annuity policyholders and are therefore unencumbered by the other obligations of the insurance company. The state (or states) running the process should allow variable annuity policyholders to continue to operate under all of the terms of the contract. The only aspect of a basic variable annuity that should be require any backing from the Guarantee Association is the guaranteed death benefit. In situations where the death benefit exceeds the value of the account value, the difference is paid out of the insurance company's general account, thereby creating a potential liability for the guarantee association. However, I suspect most policyholders will just want to get out of a failed insurance company. Sticking around to maintain a benefit that is not payable until the policyholder's death is not likely to be a priority in such a situation.

Living benefits have greatly muddied the waters in discussions about addressing bankruptcy. Like the guaranteed death benefits, the insurance company's living benefit guarantees are backed by the general account, not the separate account. Therefore, one would assume that any shortfall of these guarantees would be covered. In fact, NOLHGA's website indicates that this is indeed the case. The FAQ section states, "Generally speaking, a variable annuity contract with general account guarantees will be eligible for guaranty association coverage, subject to applicable limits and exclusions on coverage." It sounds reassuring until they go on to give themselves a way out. The very next sentence of the FAQ states the following:

"However, specific questions regarding coverage will be determined by the applicable guaranty association based on the terms of the contract, other relevant facts, and the guaranty association law in effect at the time of insolvency."

I translate that as follow: "Variable annuity living benefits are covered unless we decide they are not." The real problem here is that the statutes indicate that annuity "benefits" are covered, but the term "benefit" is undefined. Are death and living benefits true "benefits" as defined by the statute? And if so, how is the value of these benefits determined?

Let's begin by looking at this logically. Whether it is a fixed annuity or a variable annuity, the goal will be the same – don't allow policyholders to lose money. But what constitutes losing money on a living benefit? The policyholder most certainly hasn't lost any money as long as the benefit remains in the accumulation stage. Keep in mind, also, that when income starts under the benefit, initially the policyholder is simply receiving his or her own money. The client will not incur a loss until the lifetime income withdrawals deplete the account value and the insurance company is required to continue payments from its general account. Even if the living benefit is deeply in the money (the income base is significantly higher than the account value), the account value is not likely to be liquidated until ten or more years after the income begins. It seems unlikely to me that the guarantee associations are going to find it necessary to provide money to a policyholder that may or may not have a loss years down the road.

The same is true regarding any death benefits. No actual benefit is due until the designated person, usually the annuitant, dies. It seems equally unlikely to me that the guarantee association is going to provide money to cover a benefit that may or may not occur in the future. If they do choose to make good on these guarantees, they will likely require the policyholder to keep the policy in force and then pay any shortfall from these benefits out if and when it becomes necessary.

To get an idea of how this might work, we could look at company that is currently working through the rehabilitation process. Penn Treaty Network America Ins. Co. is a long-term care company (mostly) that was placed into rehabilitation by the state insurance department of Pennsylvania back in 2009. Fast-forward 10 years to 2019 and the state still has not assessed any member insurance companies to cover losses. The state has simply used Penn Treaty's existing assets to pay claims as they came due. However, as I write this, since Penn Treaty only has $700 million left in assets to cover an estimated $3+ billion in liabilities, this approach will soon come to an end. While this is a long-term care company and not a variable annuity company, the process the state followed may be instructive. Like a long-term care company, an annuity company with living benefits on the books will experience the actual losses due to the benefits over time. Even in the worst financial situation, it will be a long time until the company runs out of assets to cover the liabilities. Therefore, it will be tempting for the state insurance department to just kick the can down the road for as long as possible.

The real question could very well be will the policyholder be allowed to begin to receive or continue to receive income payments from the living benefit at all? Such income payments are really just a systematic withdrawal that is guaranteed for life (assuming the withdrawal rules are followed). As mentioned previously, the first thing the regulators typically do is suspend withdrawals. They would have to elect to make an exception for withdrawals received as a result of the living benefit. This could be even more problematic for variable annuity assets. Since variable annuity assets are part of the company's separate account, they could certainly justify this distinction. However, there could be significant political pressure on them not to make an exception. Fixed annuity policyholders are typically older, more conservative and less wealthy than variable annuity policyholders. How would it play in the press if the insurance department prohibited the 80-year-old grandmother from making a withdrawal from her fixed annuity, but allowed the 62-year-old upper middle-class variable annuity policyholder to withdraw funds without restrictions? My argument is that the proper solution would be to restrict policyholders with living benefits to just the income that is available through the living benefit. That strikes me as the logical conclusion. However, I would refer you back to the statement that *"specific questions regarding coverage will be determined by the applicable guaranty association."*

It Is impossible to predict how annuities with or without living benefits will be treated until the industry witnesses a situation where some of the theories presented in this chapter are put to the test in an actual case. With luck, that will never occur. It almost certainly will, however, and then I will most certainly need to update this chapter.

CHAPTER 17

WHY DIVORCE CAN KILL AN ANNUITY

This is going to be a brief chapter, but it is a critical one that deserves its own space for easy reference, given the problems I have seen with how annuities are often handled in divorce proceedings. Virtually every annuity company treats the splitting of an annuity that is part of a divorce decree as though a partial withdrawal is done from the annuity. These "withdrawals" can have grave consequences when it comes to taxes and product features such as living benefits. Many of these problems can be avoided if the divorce attorneys understood these problems, but sadly, very few attorneys do (or care). The insurance companies could be helpful in determining the best way to handle the annuity, but divorcing couples and their respective attorneys rarely consult them prior to the issuance of the final divorce decree. At that point, their hands are tied. Advisors that understand the potential pitfalls can help clients manage annuity contracts in divorce proceedings without incurring potential destructive financial consequences.

Acknowledge the Challenges

1. Possible Tax Consequences And Surrender Charges

Typically, the court instructs the insurance company to divide the annuity in two just like any other financial asset. The ideal solution would be for the company to retroactively issue two contracts to replace the one. Unfortunately, it is administratively difficult, if not impossible for insurance companies to do this. Not only would they have to backdate both of the new contracts to the original issue date, but they would have to establish different owners and annuitants as well. In addition, they would have to allocate the cost basis equally between the two contracts. I have found a couple of companies that can and are willing to do this, but these companies are squarely in the minority. The vast majority will effectively make a withdrawal equal to 50% of the account value and establish a second contract with a current effective date. The problem comes from the fact that unless the insurance company is willing to treat this "withdrawal" as an internal partial 1035 exchange, it will be taxable to the extent of interest earned on the contract. In addition, since the "withdrawal" is more than the 10% free withdrawal, it could be subject to surrender charges as well. Not only will this transaction effectively reduce the total value of the annuity by the amount of the surrender charges, but it will undoubtedly create an argument between the ex-spouses as to who is responsible for the taxes.

It should be noted that the insurance company will likely send the 1099 to the owner of the original contract.

2. Guaranteed Minimum Account Benefit Problems

Prior to the financial crises, variable annuity companies often offered guaranteed minimum account benefit riders (GMABs). These riders would increase the account value to the original amount invested, adjusted for withdrawals, if on the 10th anniversary the account value was less than the original amount invested. In other words, it was a guarantee of principal after 10 years. The potential problem here rests with the words "adjusted for withdrawals". This phrase typically means that the amount of the guarantee on the 10th anniversary is reduced dollar for dollar by any previous withdrawal. If the account value is $50,000 and the original amount invested was $100,000 and then a divorce decree instructs the insurance company to divide the contract in half, the $25,000 "withdrawal" that is made to fund the second contract for the other spouse, will reduce the GMAB by $25,000 as well. Therefore, the insurance company would only be required to increase the account value to $75,000 on the 10th anniversary. Had the policy not been cut in half as a result of the divorce, the insurance company would have had to increase the account $50,000 on the 10th anniversary (from $50,000 to the original $100,000). Thus, the divorce decree has potentially reduced the value of the annuity by $25,000 in addition to any surrender charges.

3. Living Benefit Problems

These complications are certainly frustrating, but the erosion in value that can be created by splitting an annuity with a living benefit – especially on a variable annuity – can be the costliest by far. For a living benefit to perform as expected, the policyholder must follow the rules and limitations of the rider. One of those limitations involves the consequences of taking an excess withdrawal. And you can certainly bet that taking a 50% "withdrawal" in order to divide an annuity in half will be considered an excess withdrawal under the terms of the living benefit rider. I covered the possible consequences of an excess withdrawal in detail in the living benefit chapter. At best, an excess withdrawal will reduce the amount of the guaranteed income for life. At worst, it will reset the income benefit back to the account value and effectively eliminate any additional income the rider would provide due to the rider being in the money. In short, this can be a very costly transaction for the remainder of both spouses' lives.

The Solution

Unless you happen to be working with one of the few insurance companies that will actually divide the contracts in half and retroactively issue the 2 new contracts back to the original issue date, two possible solutions exist to avoid the adverse consequences of splitting the contracts. The first is to get the divorce court to issue instructions to the insurance company on how to treat the contract. Faced with direct orders from the court, the insurance company will have no choice but to find a way to comply. Don't be surprised, however, if the insurance company still tries to resist the court order. Given both the administrative burden this will create for them, combined with the fact that they might benefit financially by reducing the guarantees of either the GMAB or living benefit, they might try and argue that they are bound by the terms of the contract or prospectus, or both. It's my experience that what to do in a divorce is rarely, if ever, directly addressed by either the contract or the prospectus, so you should have a firm legal position. But there is still a risk that the insurance company will choose to comply with the court order in a way that has financial consequences for both spouses.

The other solution is to not divide the contract at all. If the annuity is worth $100,000, then have one spouse keep the annuity (preferable, the current owner) and have the other spouse get an asset of equal value. I was once asked to consult on behalf of one of the spouses on a case where the husband and wife had 11 different annuities between them. Almost all of them had a living benefit. Not only did I recommend not dividing the annuities, but I listed in order of preference the annuities the spouse I was advising should keep in the event that they decided to divvy up the annuities between them. Those that had the most valuable benefits combined with the lowest possible tax consequences were put at the top of the list. Two policies of equal value may appear on the surface as though they are equal to each other, but if they are outside of retirement plans, they rarely are. A policy worth $100,000 with an $80,000 cost basis is far more valuable after taxes than a policy of the same value but has a $50,000 cost basis.

Differentiate Yourself As An Expert

Divorce is one of, if not the greatest destroyer of wealth, yet few divorce attorneys understand the possible problems they can create by dividing annuities in half. This is an area, therefore, where you can differentiate yourself from other advisors. I would suggest you meet with all of the divorce lawyers in your area and let them know that treating annuities like other assets can inadvertently reduce the wealth of both spouses. Let them know that you stand ready to advise them on any case where an annuity is involved. You and the attorney will both create value for yourselves as experts in the eyes of the divorcing spouses.

CHAPTER 18

MAKING COMPLIANCE YOUR ALLY

If only I had a dollar for every time an advisor has complained about how difficult it can be to get an annuity application approved by the firm's compliance department! And there is no doubt that the suitability oversight is much more rigorous than it was 10-20 years ago, or even five years ago. More specific FINRA supervisory rules, a steady stream of FINRA sweeps, and more than a few fines and legal losses have all caused the entire industry to be more diligent before approving an annuity application – particularly if that application is a 1035 exchange. And since annuities now always land on FINRA's annual list of "complex products," don't expect the amount of oversight to be more casual anytime soon. But that doesn't mean that compliance has to be an obstacle to using annuities in your practice. It just means that you have to understand what compliance is trying to accomplish.

Put yourself in the shoes of your annuity compliance officer. Picture an auditor asking about an annuity transaction that was done 5-10 years previously. It's highly unlikely that he will remember that particular case (and it's probably not a good thing if he or does), therefore he is going to have to rely on documentation to explain why the application was suitable. And keep in mind that if an auditor (or litigator) is asking about the case, that auditor probably already suspects that there is a good chance that something is irregular. In other words, the auditor is looking for a way to prove there is a problem. In addition, any FINRA exam or arbitration panel will likely judge the case based on a "best interests" standard even if a suitability standard was the proper requirement at the time the policy was sold. Although the industry doesn't operate from a uniform fiduciary standard, the importance of adequately documenting the transaction becomes readily apparent. I would suggest that every application should address most, if not all of the following:

1. How does this annuity fit into the client's financial plan? Be specific and complete. Saying the client is buying the annuity for tax deferral is not complete. Saying that the client is in a 30% marginal tax bracket, has fully funded her retirement plan and is looking to shelter earnings from additional taxes is complete. Adding that the annuity will help the client avoid the 3.8% investment income tax or help the client avoid an increase in her Medicare premiums, for example, is even better.

2. What is the income plan if a living benefit is being added to the annuity? A living benefit in itself is not a reason to buy an annuity. You need to have a plan on how the income from the living benefit will be used. When will the income start? What is the income need? How will the living benefit fill that income need? Why this particular living benefit rather than one from another company and/or type of annuity (i.e., an indexed annuity)? Again, be detailed and thorough. Here is an example:

Mr. Clemens is 55 years old. He expects to retire at 65. His goal is to defer taking social security until the maximum age of 70. He will therefore, need $20,000 per year in additional income beginning at age 65. The 5% growth of the living benefit's income base will guarantee at least $15,000 of the needed income – even more if there is a step up. The ability to add the living benefit rider without incurring additional investment restrictions improves the client's chances of getting more income in the future via a step up.

3. If there is an obvious alternative investment product that is not an annuity, why did you select the annuity? Keep in mind that the majority of the investment community, and most regulators, believe there is almost always a better alternative than an annuity. Therefore, it is important that you enumerate all of the ways in which an annuity will benefit a client's retirement strategy that other products cannot. The advantages are many and include tax deferral, lifetime income, access to many fund options within one product, a guaranteed death benefit, a reduction in the 3.8% investment income tax, principal protection against a rise in interest rates, creditor protection, etc. Clearly articulate the unique benefits the annuity delivers that other products cannot.

4. If you are upgrading the death benefit on a variable annuity, provide the data. What is the old death benefit and how is it calculated? What death benefit would be provided under the new contract and how is it calculated? How will any future withdrawals affect the death benefit on the new policy? Will the client have to pay more for the new death benefit? If so, how much? Most variable annuities only offer a return of premium death benefit. Therefore, if the account value is now significantly higher than this minimum death benefit, the current minimum death benefit is of little, if any value. Doing a 1035 exchange in order to step up the death benefit to the current value of the contract is a valid reason for an exchange, but you must fully document this. As a warning, the minimum death benefit on an existing policy is not always obvious by just looking at the variable annuity statement. Since the death benefit is the greater of the account value or the original investment (adjusted for withdrawals), most variable annuity companies will list the larger value as the death benefit on the statement. This can be a very different value than the minimum death benefit (which may or may not be listed on the statement). In my mind, a death benefit that drops with the account value is not a death benefit at all. It's an account value. In such a situation, the only thing the company is actually guaranteeing is the minimum death benefit.

5. If it's a 1035 exchange, how is the client benefiting from new policy vs. the existing one? Exchanges tend to be the most regulated and audited type of all annuity purchases. It is particularly important, therefore, that you clearly outline the differences between the two policies. Just saying that the new policy is cheaper or a living benefit has been added, is not sufficient. At the very least you should cover each of the following:

a. What are the cost comparisons of both policies? In addition to contract costs and rider costs, give a general description of the overall sub-account fees if it's a variable annuity. Take the time to get all of the costs of the existing contracts. If there is a rider on the policy, you will likely need to call the insurance company to get this information. The original rider fee will be listed in the contract, but that fee has likely changed since the issue date. If you are not the agent of record, get a copy of the client's statement. If you know the client's social security number, the statement will likely give you all of the information you need to get through the company's security questions. If not, you are going to have to put the client on the phone with you.

b. Why does it make sense to start a new surrender charge? Unless there are extenuating circumstances, most firms will routinely reject an exchange of an annuity that is still within the surrender charge period. Therefore, I will limit my comments here to exchanges out of contracts that are beyond the surrender charge period. This means you are moving from an annuity that is not only totally liquid, but you will be starting a new charge on the current account value. You will need to clarify several points to complete this transaction. When will the client need to access the money? Will those withdrawals fall within the free withdrawal amount or be beyond the surrender charge period? What other liquid funds are available if there is an unexpected need for liquidity? If you are going to try to exchange a policy that is still in the surrender charge period, you must demonstrate how the higher expected returns, death benefit or living benefit income guarantees of the new contract will recover the surrender charge and then some. If you cannot demonstrate that, don't even bother to submit the exchange for approval.

c. <u>What does the new annuity offer that the old one doesn't?</u> Keep in mind that most regulators assume financial advisors help clients do 1035 exchanges to earn a commission. For that reason, there will be a bias against the new annuity. Your compliance people will understand this. So, they will want a specific reason or two (or three) as to what the new contract offers that the old one does not. Valid reasons would include lower fees, better or more varied sub-accounts, the addition of a living benefit, the ability to lock in a higher return of premium death benefit and/or a better crediting method (if it's an indexed annuity). If you are adding a living benefit, then you will need to explain why the client didn't need a living benefit when the original contract was purchased and why they do now. If you are dropping a living benefit that is no longer needed, explain why the guaranteed income provided by the old contract is no longer necessary. In other words, how has the client's objectives changed since the original contract was purchased?

d. <u>What is the client giving up by getting rid of the current contract</u> <u>and why is that not as important as what the client is gaining?</u> Most annuity suitability forms ask you to articulate the "cons" of the 1035. Don't ever list "none". The client is giving up something even if it's just the better liquidity that the original contract almost certainly has (even if you are moving to a c-share or a no-load in a fee-based account, the client is likely paying more for the same level of liquidity). If you don't show a thorough understanding of what the client is giving up, the compliance department is going to be skeptical about your other statements throughout the document.

The Concentration Issue

FINRA guidance states that no client should ever be over concentrated in annuities. Unfortunately, they do not define or describe what would constitute an over concentration. In addition, the guidance does not differentiate different types of annuities or even annuities with or without surrender charges. Consequently, most firms set a concentration limit that typically ranges from 30%-50% of either net worth or liquid net worth. Obviously, no client should ever be too heavily weighted in any product – including annuities. Unfortunately, these restrictions tend to be too broad and vague. In my view, that could work to your advantage. While a specific rule (i.e., "no client can have more than 33.6% of their net worth in annuities.") might be simpler and less confusing, one size fits all rules often lead to results that defy logic. Therefore, we will likely have to continue to live with this confusing issue.

In my view, there are valid reasons to allow an annuity concentration beyond the typical limits. Some of the more obvious reasons are as follows:

1. Currently held annuities that are out of surrender charges. If a client currently owns annuities that have no surrender charges and are therefore essentially liquid, I believe those annuities should carry less weight towards the concentration limit. Obviously, the tax implications of non-qualified annuities can make these contracts one of the last places you would go for an unexpected liquidity need, but if tax implications are enough to classify an investment as illiquid, many types of investments would be equally illiquid. Unfortunately, FINRA deems all annuities, even those with no surrender charges, as illiquid assets. While I believe that this defies logic, it's the reality under which your compliance department must work.

2. Fixed annuities are being used as a CD alternative. The goal of these annuities is to provide a higher return than other investments that are considered safe. Clients typically understand that they are going to pay a penalty or charge to get out of any of these investments before maturity. While this doesn't make the annuity liquid, it is important to look at relative liquidity to other alternative investments. As an example, in many cases getting out of an annuity early would be less costly than getting out of a Certificate of Deposit. With that in mind, why prohibit a client from buying a fixed or indexed annuity just because she already has a significant portion of her portfolio in annuities?

3. Immediate annuities that are used to meet an income gap. If the client needs a specific amount of income and an immediate annuity is the best alternative to achieve this goal, such annuities need to be looked at differently. It makes little sense to tell the client, "Yes, I know you need $20,000 in annual income and I know an immediate annuity will give you that amount of income with the least amount of capital, but this purchase would put you over my firm's concentration limit so I can only give you some of the income you need." The reality is that some clients may need to annuitize a significant percentage of their investible assets in order to provide the guaranteed lifetime income they need in retirement. In fact, academic studies indicate the most efficient retirement portfolio allocation for some savers — particularly those with between $400,000 and $2 million — could call for as much as 40-50% of the portfolio to be allocated to either an immediate annuity or a combination of an immediate annuity and deferred income annuity.[1] Prohibiting those clients from doing that simply because the required percentage is greater than a company guideline makes little financial sense.

I understand why, as an advisor, you might recognize reasons to submit an annuity order that will put your client over your firm's limits. Just know that such a tactic will raise questions, given deeply ingrained biases surrounding annuities. You need to provide clear and specific reason as to why this case warrants such an exception.

---

[1] https://www.advisorperspectives.com/articles/2015/08/04/why-bond-funds-don-t-belong-in-retirement-portfolios

Some Thoughts About Advisory Annuities

The reality is that regulators have such a heavy focus on annuity recommendations because they are concerned that too many annuities are sold mostly so that the agent can earn a "high" commission. This is also why 1035 exchanges carry the most scrutiny. Regulators are concerned that the replacement recommendation is more about earning a new commission than giving the client a better annuity. Think about all of the data points that compliance departments collect in order to review an annuity trade. It's mostly about fees and surrender charges – all of which are highly correlated to the size of the commission. The higher the commission, the higher the annual fees and/or surrender charges.

So, what does that mean for the growing number of advisory annuities – none of which pay a commission, all of which have significantly lower fees and most of which don't have a surrender charge (some advisory indexed annuities carry a small surrender charge in order to help cover hedging costs)? When an annuity is sold within an advisory account, the advisor will not earn any more money on the annuity than any other investment product. Therefore, that advisor is completely unconflicted. I would argue that such a recommendation should not carry any more supervisory oversight than any other product. Other than a need to have additional disclosures around the complexity of the annuity, why should an advisory annuity recommendation require more paperwork than a mutual fund or a unit investment trust? And yet, firms continue to supervise them as if they are a commissionable annuity.

And absent guidance from the regulators to the contrary, compliance departments are not likely to change that stance any time soon.

Take Away

If you walk away from this chapter with only one thing in mind it should be that when it comes to annuity documentation, more is better. It is virtually impossible to give too much information to the person reviewing the trade. The reality is, the more you articulate your plan, the more faith your compliance person will have that you are making a thoughtful and measured investment decision. Avoid short and incomplete responses. Following is a list of reasons that are most likely to make compliance cringe. Over the years, I have seen all of these short and unspecific reasons given to justify an annuity purchase. Ask yourself if you would approve the application based solely on one or more of the following:

1. "Lower cost"
2. "Better death benefit"
3. "Guaranteed income"
4. "No longer needs a living benefit"
5. "Better investment returns" (As if the new annuity come with a crystal ball!)
6. "An index annuity better meets the clients risk profile"

Sadly, compliance professionals come across explanations like these, lacking in substance and details, every day. I know it takes time to provide the documentation suggested in this chapter. However, if it gets the order approved on the first try, you are likely to spend less time in the long run if you do it right to begin with.

How You Can Help Yourself If a Trade is Questioned After Issue?

Your compliance person is not the only person that needs to be concerned about how well a trade is documented should someone later question the suitability of the trade. Obviously, you have a vested interest in this as well. You don't want to be in front of an arbitration panel struggling to explain why you sold a particular annuity and how it works. With that in mind, I offer the following suggestions:

1. Document every meeting you had with the client about the annuity. Keep copies of <u>all of your notes and any calculations</u> you did to determine the suitability of the trade.
2. Put a copy of the original prospectus and/or client brochure in the client's file. Variable annuity companies frequently change the terms, costs and features of their products. Fixed and indexed companies frequently discontinue products and replace them with new ones. Finding someone at the insurance company who can give you the relevant information on an old contract can be very difficult. And it is not uncommon to get wrong information when they do try to help you. After all, the service rep that takes your phone call most likely wasn't around when the original annuity was sold. Having an original

document to refer to will likely save you a significant amount of time down the road.

3. If you are recommending a variable annuity and your firm subscribes to Morningstar's Annuity Intelligence report, print out the report on the particular product you sold at the time you sold it. The report allows you to select any riders that were added to the policy, thereby giving you a complete description of how the rider works and what it costs. Keep this report in the client's file. It will be the best possible reference source years down the road.

4. Keep a copy of the initial confirm or client statement. This will give you all of the information you need on how the policy was initiated.

One final word of advice: If you have a case that you think is likely to attract a more intense level of compliance review than others, pick up the phone and call your compliance professional. If you work for an advisor-centric firm, he or she will be more than happy to discuss the case with you in advance of you going through the effort to complete the paperwork, or worse yet, actually recommend an annuity to a client that is subsequently declined.

If you are thinking that this type of documentation is a lot of work, you won't get any arguments from me. It clearly is. But as more firms embrace the fiduciary standard as an accepted practice, this type of documentation will become the norm for all recommendations.

ABOUT THE AUTHOR

Scott Stolz, CFP®, RICP® has been one of the most influential people in the annuity industry for almost four decades. Over that time, he held senior marketing, sales and operational roles for three major annuity providers. Since 2005, he has served as the President of Raymond James Insurance Group – one of the  industry's largest annuity distributors. Scott's diverse responsibilities have given him a front-row seat to virtually every pivotal period that has led the annuity industry to where it is today. Starting with the Baldwin United rehabilitation process in the 80's, to the development of the industry's first multi-manager variable annuity in the early 90's, to the rollout of one of the industry's first indexed annuities in the mid 90's and the most recent DOL Fiduciary Rule; Scott has led or been involved in at all stages.

Scott's broad and unique background makes him ideally suited to author such a practical, no-nonsense handbook on annuities. Whether you consistently recommend annuities or just want to know the real story about where annuities fit in a portfolio and where they don't, this book is the one you should have on your shelf.

Made in the USA
Columbia, SC
08 March 2022

57385745R00143